# Business Casual Made Easy

## The Complete Guide to Business Casual Dress for Men and Women

By Ilene Amiel and Angie Michael

Business Casual Publications, L.C.

**Business Casual Made Easy**
The Complete Guide to Business Casual Dress for Men and Women
By Ilene Amiel and Angie Michael

Illustrations by Diane Russell
Text design by Joyce C. Weston

Published by Business Casual Publications, L.C.
7804 Wincanton Court, Falls Church, VA 22043

For Additional Information:
Amiel (914) 478-3827
Michael (703) 560-3950

Copyright © 1999 by Ilene Amiel and Angie Michael
First Printing, November 1999

Library of Congress Catalog Card Number: 99-0945597
ISBN 0-9672878-0-4

Printed in the United States of America

This book is available at quantity discounts when used to promote products or services. For information call (914) 478-3827.

Visit our web site at www.businesscasualdress.com

# Contents

# Acknowledgments

THANK YOU VERY MUCH!

Writing this book has been a journey for both of us. We worked hard in the midst of personal and professional challenges, and we also learned and laughed while compiling and developing the ideas for our book. This project was possible thanks to the great support we have received from our families, friends, clients, and colleagues. We want to especially thank Suzan Nanfeldt, our dear friend and colleague who started working with Angie on this project in 1995. In 1997 she worked with Ilene on the same idea, and finally paved the way for both of us to connect and continue the work she helped initiate. Suzan, we appreciate your ideas, your encouragement, and your great faith in our project.

The survey of 165 top executives from around the country was possible thanks to the cooperation of our dear friends and colleagues from the Association of Image Consultants International. We thank you for your willingness to interview your corporate clients and for your diligence in completing the questionnaires. Thanks, dear friends!

Sidney Bayne
Georgette Braadt
Allie Casey
Jean Gaffney
Kathleen Golden
Lynne Henderson
Gwen Mazer
Nancy Penn
Elaine Stoltz
Jean Mestress Sulc

Mary Jane Barnes
Denise Butchko
Debbie Leaper
Marion Gellatly
Holly Horning
Maggie McQuown
Patricia Nasser
Penny Pilafas
Valerie Sokolosky

Thanks to the immensely talented people who made this book special and were a joy to work with. Our book cover designer, George Foster, who was extremely patient while making numerous cover drafts for the two "most difficult to please" authors.

Diane Russell, our creative illustrator. You did a great job in designing the clothing and accessories illustrations that made our book so unique.

Thanks to the people behind the scenes. Our research consultant, Diana Merkel, our editor, Pam Leigh, our text designer, Joyce Weston and Angie's Office Manager, Keri Nikol.

Thanks to Carol Hyatt and the participants from the Leadership Forum for their support and encouragement to Ilene all along the way.

Thanks to our clients who encouraged us to write this book and to our seminar participants who signaled what was really important for the books content. We hope that this book will be the guide you asked for.

Then, there are those very special people close to our hearts who patiently supported us before, during, and after this project. Our families! Steven Amiel, Ilene's husband, we thank you for your support, your ideas, and for making the printing of our book a painless experience. Alex and Travis Amiel, Ilene's sons, your smiles and laughs, even when mommy was at the computer with another deadline, will be in our gratitude corner forever.

George Michael, Angie's husband known as Mr. Wonderful, we appreciate your unconditional love and support through this project and for your honest feedback when we needed a reality check to ensure that our readers would understand our suggestions on casual clothing.

To all of you, many thanks!

# Introduction

As we approach the millennium, corporate America continues to change with the new technology and the relaxed and easy way of doing business. Casual business attire is being adopted across the country by everyone in small firms to large corporations. Business casual is replacing traditional business attire as the norm for many Americans.

Business casual policies seem to be a great benefit for employees who are delighted with the freedom to wear casual, more relaxed clothes to work. However, many organizations and individuals complain that there is *confusion* about what is or is not appropriate to wear to work.

Traditional business attire was predictable and safe. It included symbols easy to identify and easy to exemplify. You put on a suit with a shirt and tie or with a blouse, added classic accessories, and you were ready to do business anywhere. Now, with the new trend of business casual, employees have to make many more choices. Choices give more freedom, but they also cause confusion. The biggest challenge seems to be how to select casual clothes that are still professional and appropriate for work.

Many executives tell us that when they meet to discuss budgets or any other business-related issues, their meetings are predictable and manageable. But when they meet to define a casual dress policy for their organization, they stumble. Everyone at the table has a different interpretation of business casual. Some people think business casual means khakis and polo shirts, others think jeans and T-shirts, and many think a jacket is still required. Some insist that exercise gear with sneakers or sandals are just as appropriate for the office.

What is really business casual? What is appropriate to wear to work? This confusion and the feedback from our participants in our seminars motivated us to write this book. Our intent is to clarify to individuals and organizations what business casual is, what it is not, and how to select casual clothing while maintaining professionalism and credibility.

This book started many years ago when we both began assisting organizations and individuals in making choices for business casual. We have worked with numerous organizations in defining appropriate dress codes and policies that are easy to implement and follow. We have taught seminars to hundreds of people around the country on how to select business casual for their specific position, region, and industry.

Based on our experiences and research, we realized the need to offer our information to many other organizations and to the millions of Americans that have the same questions. What should I wear to work? What is appropriate business casual attire for my position?

This book is a response to all the questions you and your organization have about business casual. What it is. What it is not. How to create an outfit that is more casual. How to select casual clothes that are appropriate for your industry and your position. When it is still necessary to wear traditional business attire. What to wear to visit a client, to make a presentation, to travel, and so forth.

The most significant contribution of our book is our definition of three distinct levels of business casual: *Classic, Smart, and Relaxed.* You will find a complete description of each level, their characteristics, key times, the perception that it creates, and the situations for when each one is appropriate. These levels will provide you with the answers of what to wear when.

We also have identified those items of clothing and accessories that seem most controversial. Many organizations consider these items appropriate while others definitely don't want to see their employees wearing them. With the collaboration of a group of our colleagues, we conducted a survey of 165 top executives around the country from different industries. We asked them for their opinion about the appropriateness of these controversial items, and we have presented the data according to industries and regions. This data will be a great resource for you in choosing your attire when dealing with clients from either your industry or a different industry. It will also be useful if your organization has not defined a specific dress code.

You will find a chapter with guidelines on how to dress for special situations, travel, entertainment, and job interviewing. There are chapters with tips and suggestions on clothing fit and care, wardrobe management, and resources that will help you to save money and time. If you are in human resources or if you are a manager involved in designing and implementing a dress code policy, you will find a complete chapter on this subject to simplify your task.

As you will see, this book is a *how-to* manual that you can pick up at any point to find answers to any question related to business casual. From dressing appropriately for a regular day at the office, making presentations, meeting with clients, negotiating, to defining a business casual policy for your organization.

With this book we want to assure you that business casual is a benefit for you and for your organization and that it is easy!

Angie and Ilene

# Business Casual: Dressing for the New Millennium

*As we enter the twenty-first century, dressing to impress is less
important than dressing for efficiency and flexibility!*

### First Impressions for the New Millennium

In the informational age of *"high tech and low touch,"* face-to-face interactions are becoming less frequent and brief. Computers and phones
lessen the need for as much in-person business contact. On those occa-
sions when a personal meeting is required, however, how we present our-
selves is still important, although the rules are changing rapidly. Just as
faxes and e-mail largely have replaced formal business letters as the pre-
ferred way to correspond, traditional business attire is being replaced by
business casual clothing.

First impressions may no longer be a face-to-face experience. They start
before we even meet through the newer mediums of e-mail, video con-
ferencing, and Web sites. When it finally comes, the personal encounter
either confirms or changes our "electronic" impression. Visual elements
now count for 55% of your message; your spoken or written words,
which are weighted at almost 100% without face-to-face contact, now
account for only 7% of your communication; and your tone of voice
counts for 38%.

We are now judged by different criteria for credibility, professionalism, creativity, confidence, and approachability. Impressing is out, empowerment and flexibility are in.

*Suits and khakis are having a meeting, and the suit is not necessarily the boss.*

*A twin-sweater set is at the table with a double-breasted skirted suit, and the sweater set is presenting the more valuable ideas. No one is surprised anymore! Being comfortable does not conflict with being in charge.*

As corporate America continues to evolve, the hard-and-fast rules that once governed the traditional nine-to-five workplaces are bending, and with them the ways American workers dress for business. For generations, the standards of attire for America's office workers were unchanged. Men and women were expected to wear dark suits or serious jackets in conservative colors and designs. As corporate America embraces casual clothes as the norm for business attire, traditional business suits become the exception. A suit is taken out for presentations, meetings with clients, or closing deals.

Organizational culture and work attire have definitely changed, and our society likes the change. In the nineties, advances in technology and increased competition made downsizing, among other management strategies, a common solution for coping with the rapid changes in the marketplace. Corporations are being reengineered so they are flexible and adaptable, ready to take on the changes that are inevitable.

The new business environment calls for different values, behavior, and dress. Choices, creativity, team spirit, a relaxed working atmosphere, relaxed work schedules, and relaxed clothing are the new rules of the office. Flex-time, job sharing, paternity leave, summer hours, home offices, and outsourcing are among the responses to this new business environment. The switch from traditional business attire to business casual is in sync with the new organization's "very nonrule-oriented culture."

Corporate casualness is a sign of the changing times. It reflects in part the rise of jean-clad baby boomers to positions of authority. In a society where denim is a way of life and strangers address each other by first names, it's only natural that relaxed attire would finally enter the workplace.

If one believes that dressing down results in being happier, more productive, and more creative, then one's behavior will bear that out. How one dresses has always been linked to how one behaves, hence the expression "Clothes make the man (or woman)." The way you look affects the way you think, feel, and act. Health care practitioners have long observed that renewed attention to appearance is a sign of recovery in depressed patients.

Managers are empowering employees to choose work clothes from a variety of styles, fabrics, and colors. Many management consultants think that by giving employees the option to dress casually, companies are demonstrating their commitment and concern for the well-being of their employees.

Organizations are reporting such positive benefits from allowing relaxed work attire, that business casual is now part of the dress code policy at most organizations. It is certainly here to stay. Clothing manufacturers, retailers and industry organizations have called business casual the single most fundamental change in how people dress for the office in this century and many predict that as we enter the year 2000, half of all U.S. corporations will allow business casual dress on a full-time basis. *Women's Wear Daily*, the bible of the apparel industry, has called this trend "the most radical change in career fashions since the 1970s when women began wearing slacks to work."

## Where and Who: The Start of the Business Casual Trend

### Business Casual Was Born...

A public relations executive from New York said that business casual started in Hawaii, but the Hawaiian Chamber of Commerce claims otherwise. Hawaiian businesses have long had Aloha Friday when men and women wear colorful outfits, but it is more a lifestyle than a corporate decision, they affirm.

Like many trends, it's generally conceded that casual days started first on the West Coast, where computer companies realized that allowing employees to wear jeans and short sleeves could encourage creativity in a way that suits and ties could not. High-profile Silicon Valley has given legitimacy to this low-key look. The high-tech, start-up companies were notorious for being populated by "computer geeks" who wandered the halls wearing shorts, T-shirts, and sneakers. The absence of ties is often linked in many people's minds with creativity and imagination. The Silicon Valley computer whizzes proved that employees could be productive and creative even while dressing casually. The trend made its way across, down, and throughout the country.

Others insist that the casual workday trend started in 1990 in Canada when many companies introduced a dress-down day as part of their annual United Way campaigns. The idea of generating United Way contributions by asking office workers to pay for the privilege of dressing casually was an instant success. This fund-raising idea soon moved to the United States with grand results. For example, in the state of Delaware, 67 companies and 2,400 workers participated in a campaign in the early 1990s. For a $5 donation, employees were allowed to "dress down" the last Friday before summer, raising almost $20,000. Similar campaigns in the country raised over $2 million dollars in a year. Since then, the practice of wearing less formal attire, both regularly or occasionally, has swept the American workplace.

Many others attribute the business casual trend to the growing number of white-collar female professionals. As women moved into powerful positions and adopted pants, their subordinates followed their lead. Congresswomen Carole Moseley-Braun from Illinois and Barbara Mikulski from Maryland paved the way for a more relaxed Senate dress code in 1993 when they lobbied for the right to wear pantsuits on the Senate floor. Previously women had had to wear dresses or skirts and jackets. Even First Lady Hillary Rodham Clinton has made speeches and other public appearances in pantsuits.

Conservative corporations popularized relaxed attire by allowing middle managers to attend off-site seminars dressed in sport coats, polo shirts, and khaki pants. The response was so positive that the managers wanted to bring the same relaxed comfort from the off-site sessions to the office.

Retailers have promoted casual wear for the past ten years, which some retail analysts say is all about increasing profits by creating customer demand for new clothing. In particular, analysts say retailers are trying to persuade male buyers to shop more than twice a year by creating a need for more sweaters, sport pants, and shirts. To convince men that khaki pants can be worn for work, Levi Strauss & Co. spent millions on an advertising campaign showing men wearing casual clothes while carrying briefcases and leading meetings.

Regardless of who or what started the business casual trend, it is here to stay. American corporations increasingly are accepting casual attire as the norm for business wear, either daily or occasionally.

# The Four Cs of Business Casual: Advantages and Disadvantages

*"Casual dress is the only employee benefit that doesn't cost anything—not a cent—and it seems to be the one that gets the most applause,"* is a common sentiment among corporate executives. In addition to being a cheap morale booster, there is a growing assumption among organizations that casual attire reaps other positive benefits as well.

The way employees dress on the job can affect the way they feel even though there is no statistical evidence that dressing down increases corporate profits or productivity. Most employees want to dress casually for work, and companies are looking for ways to boost morale and keep their employees happy.

High-tech companies want to increase sales, and they don't care how their sales force dresses as long as they meet their sales quotas. This attitude also holds true for many other companies whose employees do not have direct visual contact with customers.

Some of the greatest benefits of business casual can be described with four Cs.

**Comfort**—Being comfortable is an American value. At a time when leisure is at a premium, anything that brings comfort is welcome. Americans created the jean culture, and baby boomers and generation Xers brought it from the playroom to the boardroom. Because these two generations grew up in jeans and T-shirts, they are used to this clothing "language" and its attendant comfort, low maintenance, and low cost. Business casual attire echoes this relaxed feeling and allows for ease of movement. Comfort is the end result that Americans treasure.

**Creativity** – Some behavioral scientists have concluded that a tieless neck makes for a creative head. When you are comfortable, you feel good. And when you are not preoccupied with yourself and your clothes, your mind is freer to be creative and to pay closer attention to others. Ideas flow and are respected for their value and practicality, not by the packaging of the presenter.

**Communication** – When people are dressed in comfortable clothing—and not power suits—it invites freer communication. It lowers the barriers that titles and hierarchy can impose. Employees feel more comfortable making suggestions to a boss who's not wearing a suit. "It just feels easier to roll up your sleeves and get down to work with your managers, who look more like your colleagues than your supervisors," claim many employees. Friendliness, openness, and approachability all seem to expand when the dress code relaxes.

**Camaraderie** – Casual attire is a great equalizer. The corporate uniform symbolizes formality, power, and rigidity. Like a sports team's uniform, business casual offers a way to level the "playing field," and allows each employee to feel part of a unified team with equal value and equal responsibility for the common goal.

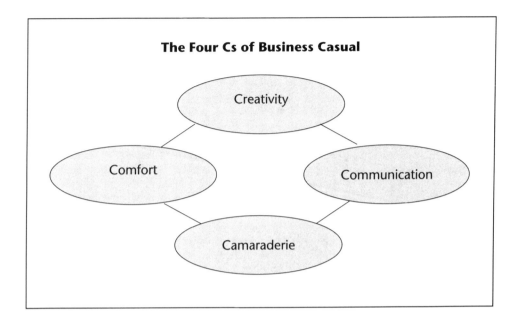

**The Four Cs of Business Casual**

Creativity

Comfort

Communication

Camaraderie

## Advantages and Disadvantages of Business Casual
## Not Everyone Thinks the Same
## The Cheers and the Tears

Since the effects of casual attire on business have not been measured, there are still conflicting opinions about its benefits and limitations for individuals and organizations. Some see the trend of business casual as a way to boost employee morale and increase productivity; others see it as an excuse for being sloppy and adversely affecting the corporate image and the level of professionalism in the workplace.

Below are some of the pros (cheers) and cons (tears) to the dress casual policy in today's workplace.

## CHEERS: Organizations

- Casual dress improves morale. Many believe that allowing casual dress garners clear advantages to the organizational culture at virtually no cost to employers. Business casual is the least expensive employee benefit.

- Casual dress policies can attract new employees. Offering casual dress and a more relaxed organizational atmosphere are attractive perks for new hires.

- Many think that allowing employees to wear casual clothing improves productivity. Work can be stressful, and a casual dress policy encourages a more relaxed, friendly, and team-oriented environment.

- Surveys conducted by Levi Strauss & Co. and other firms report that most organizations find that their employees prefer casual business attire. By implementing casual dress policies, companies show that they are *listening* to their employees.

- Organizations believe that allowing casual dress at work facilitates communications between blue- and white-collar workers. When obvious distinctions between employees are eliminated, everyone becomes an equal part of the team.

## CHEERS: Individuals

- Casual wear costs a lot less than traditional business clothing. There are also fewer dry cleaning bills and other maintenance costs.

- Casual clothing helps break down status symbols and makes it easier for people to feel like they are part of a team. Because everyone appears equal, competition decreases and communications are enhanced.

- Business casual is empowering. Management is giving employees the freedom to choose what to wear. Employees feel that business casual gives them more opportunities to be creative with their attire.

- Business casual helps create a friendly, more relaxed, and less stressful work atmosphere. It promotes teamwork and fosters creative thinking. Employees feel that they are now more valued for their contributions and ideas.

- As female executives have secured their place in the corporate hierarchy, they have become more relaxed about their business clothing choices. Many women welcome the chance to select clothing that suits their personality. They can exercise their creativity, including wearing a wide range of colors and more feminine styles.

## TEARS: Organizations

- Some organizations do not have dress code policies for business casual. Others have policies that are too general and lack specific definitions of acceptable attire. As a result, some employees are taking casual dress to an extreme by wearing weekend or beachwear to work, which can adversely affect the company's image and therefore the bottom line.

- Upper management still tends to wear higher quality, more expensive clothing, which can maintain the gap between managers and staffers.

- When employees relax their attire, they tend to get too relaxed about their work. Some companies fear that if their employees become too sloppy in their dress, they might become too casual about their work habits as well. When employees show up in cut-off jeans, wrinkled T-shirts, tank tops, sweatshirts, and so forth, their customers or clients might be hesitant to entrust their life savings, legal matters, and business to them.

- Some organizations report that some of their upper managers resist dressing in casual work clothes. For example, some organizations that have a United Way casual day to collect donations for the annual campaign, have found that while many of their employees do dress very casually that day, many managers, who still make a donation, don't.

■ Due to a lack of clear guidelines, business casual dress policies require supervision. "It is probably a good idea, but too difficult to manage," is a common claim among managers. It is difficult to outline what is and isn't appropriate.

## TEARS: Individuals

■ "For every professional who feels more productive in casual attire, there is another who feels less confident and less professionally dressed," says Susan Bixler in her book *The New Professional Image.*

■ Some women and minorities are concerned about losing their visual credibility when they wear casual clothes. Their suit enhances their authority and confidence. Wearing casual clothes at work affects women differently than men. A man in a short-sleeved shirt is perceived differently than a woman in a short-sleeved shirt. For women, showing more skin means increased vulnerability.

■ Employees need to pay more attention to their business casual attire because these clothes require extra creativity and coordination. Casual clothes reveal more about your taste and personality than a business suit.

■ Many employees complain that now they need two business wardrobes. Some low-paid female workers claim that they can't afford the type of casual clothing that higher-paid female employees wear, and feel that this dress code further diminishes their status at the office.

■ Some managers take longer to command the same respect and performance from their employees. Your credibility is now on its own and not based on or protected by your attire.

While there is still disagreement on whether business casual is good for employees and businesses, almost everyone agrees that this trend is not going away.

We can say that the dress down trend is generally regarded as more bene-
ficial than harmful. The proof is the increased number of companies that
are implementing a partial or a total casual dress policy for their organizations.

We can also see, as many organizations and individuals complain, that
*there is confusion* about what is or is not appropriate to wear to work. This
confusion motivated us to write this book. In the next chapters you will
find the answers to all your questions about business casual. What it is,
how and when to select it, and how to wear it while maintaining your
professionalism and credibility.

# Business Casual: The Meaning "A Merger of Clothing"

What exactly is business casual? What does the term mean?

When we think of *business clothing,* our mind visualizes the traditional clothing pieces connected to business attire. For men this means suits, ties, and white shirts. For women this means neutral colored skirted suits and pumps with thin soles. These are the clothes that we typically wear when we use our professional skills.

When we think of *casual clothing,* our mind imagines jeans, T-shirts, weekend wear, and comfortable shoes. These are the clothes that we wear at home and during our leisure time when we are most relaxed and at ease.

To further understand the meaning of business casual, let's picture a continuum of clothing styles ranging from the most formal and dressy on one end to the most relaxed or casual on the other. "Dressy" clothing is formal, tailored, and constructed, and consists of suits, ties, dark to medium colors, and fine fabrics. This look conveys credibility and professionalism. At the other end of the continuum we have "Casual" clothes that are comfortable, loose, relaxed, and unconstructed. Examples include T-shirts, shorts, jeans, and tennis shoes. This kind of clothing provides maximum comfort and allows for more personal creativity.

## Business Casual = A Merger of Clothing

**One Extreme
Business Clothing =**
Formal, constructed, tailored
Suits, ties, white and blue shirts
Dark and neutral colors
Thin-sole shoes

**Other Extreme
Casual Clothing =**
Relaxed, loose, colorful
T-shirts, jeans
Colorful pieces
Tennis shoes, sandals

**Business Casual
combines**
the *professionalism* of the
business look and the *comfort* of
the casual look.

**Business first; casual second**

"Business Casual" then is the combination or *merger* of these two types of attire—business and casual. To create this look, we borrow the professionalism and credibility of the business look and combine it with the comfort and creativity of casual clothing.

**One Extreme**
**Business Clothing=**
Formal, constructed, tailored
Suits, ties, white and blue shirts,
Dark and neutral colors
Thin-sole shoes

## Traditional Business Clothing

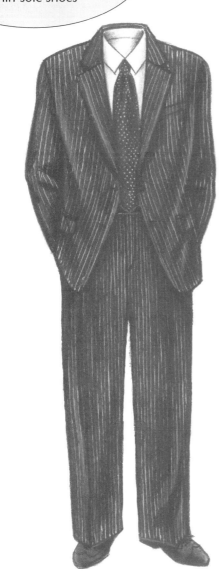

**Other Extreme Casual Clothing =**
Relaxed, loose, colorful
T-shirts, jeans
Colorful pieces
Tennis shoes, sandals

## Casual Clothing

**Business Casual combines** the *professionalism* of the business look and the *comfort* of the casual look.

## Business Casual = A Merger of Clothing

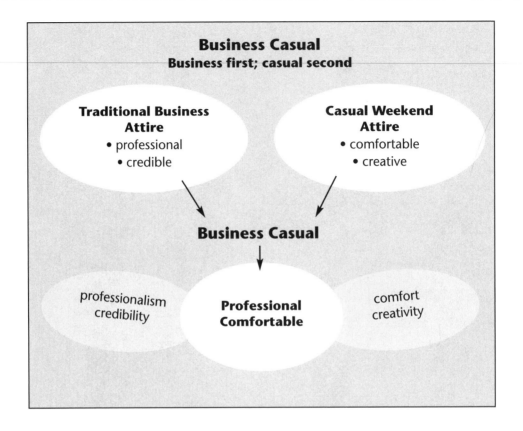

## Selecting Clothing That Is Both Business and Casual

### The Challenge

When people are permitted to wear business casual, the clothing choices are almost unlimited, which allows for increased opportunities for personal expression. But having many more options also can lead to confusion and clothing mistakes. "What is appropriate?" "What should I wear?" "Can I go to the office tomorrow in jeans and a T-shirt?" These are some of the questions facing employees who now have the opportunity to dress more casually for work, sometimes on a daily basis.

With this new clothing freedom we began to see an increase in fashion mistakes that are affecting employees and their organizations' professionalism. The problem often starts with companies announcing a new policy of "business casual" without giving clear guidelines as to what they mean by it. Even when a company does issue written guidelines, it usually doesn't cover all the situations that can occur in business.

*Does one policy fit all?* The answer is No! There is not a simple list that describes the appropriate business casual attire, and we cannot expect one that will be appropriate for all companies, all levels within the company, and for all regions in the country. Therefore it is important to recognize that whether you are dressing casual for a designated Casual Day at the office, for everyday business because that is the accepted dress code in your company, or for an office picnic, the rule of thumb is that business casual is generally more comfortable, less structured, and achieved with softer fabrics and looser silhouettes. However, you need to keep in mind several considerations when deciding what to wear: your company, your position, your customers, the occasion, the geographic location, the climate, and so forth.

Then, which garments will you choose? Do you put on your jeans and T-shirt? Or your khakis and polo shirt or shorts and tank top? Or do you put on your jacket and tie, your suit and blouse?

## The Solution!

The answers to the questions of what to wear for business casual while still retaining your professionalism start by reviewing each workday's agenda. Determine who you will be seeing and interacting with. Based on this agenda, you can choose an appropriate business casual look.

In deciding which clothing to select to be appropriate, professional, and comfortable, it helps to clarify what makes an outfit more casual.

## What Makes an Outfit More Casual?

The first step in selecting your business casual clothing is to determine whether an outfit is casual. Then, you can determine whether the outfit is also professional. When you can determine these two characteristics, the outfit belongs in your business casual wardrobe.

---

**WHAT MAKES AN OUTFIT MORE CASUAL?**

These are the key elements:

| | |
|---|---|
| **Color:** | More color and creative combinations |
| **Fabric:** | More texture, patterns, prints |
| **Layers:** | More than one item on top, more layers |
| **Construction:** | Unconstructed, loose silhouettes |
| **Accessories:** | Matte finish, ethnic, colorful |

---

## COLOR

*More Color Options.* Business casual clothing contains standard neutral colors, non-traditional colors, and creative combinations. Colors are divided into three categories:

**Neutral** – These are colors that provide for a great variety of combinations. They are non-memorable colors and mix well with many other colors. They are the foundation of a business wardrobe.

### Neutral colors

| | | | |
|---|---|---|---|
| gray | taupe | beige | navy |
| black | khaki | brown | |

**Basic** – These colors are blue, red, green, and their variations. They are not as versatile as the neutrals, but they can be combined with other shades. When used in large amounts, they can make an outfit more casual. For example, a periwinkle dress is more casual than a navy dress. A forest green blazer is more casual than a camel one.

### Basic colors

| | | | |
|---|---|---|---|
| red | burgundy | green | forest green |
| blue | royal blue | purple | teal |
| periwinkle | | | |

**Accent** – These are either brighter or lighter colors. They mix well with neutrals and basics. If used for main pieces or in large amounts, these colors can make an outfit more casual. A bright yellow sweater is more casual than a navy sweater.

### Accent colors

| | | | |
|---|---|---|---|
| orange | bright yellow | lime green | light pink |
| fuchsia | turquoise | hot pink | coral pink |
| coral | | | |

## Creative Combinations

Creative combinations are achieved by combining basic colors with accent colors. For example, red (basic) and yellow (accent) or green (basic) and orange (accent). Combining a neutral shade with two accent colors makes the outfit more casual.

Examples:

### Men

*Traditional Business Combination:*
Navy pants with white and burgundy-striped shirt

*Creative Combination:*
Navy pants with blue, white, and yellow-striped shirt
Khaki pants with purple, yellow, and red plaid shirt

### Women

*Traditional Business Combination:*
Navy blue skirted suit with white jewel neck blouse

*Creative Combination:*
Royal blue pants and sweater with yellow and
    purple pattern
Khaki pants and orange top

## FABRIC

The qualities of the fabric that affect the level of dressiness are: the texture, the pattern, and the print.

### Texture

The more texture a fabric has, the more casual the outfit becomes. Textured fabric can be described as rough, nubby, heavy, or loosely woven. Low-textured fabrics such as gabardine are finer, tightly woven, smoother. A broadcloth, which is the most common fabric used for men's shirts, has little texture, whereas a cable sweater in wool has more texture. The more textured the fabric, the more casual the garment. A tweed jacket is more casual than a wool gabardine jacket. Knits, sweaters, corduroys, and denim have more texture, which makes the outfit more casual.

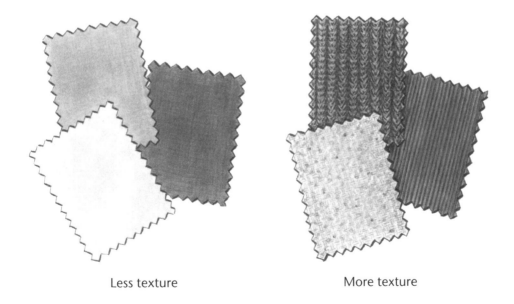

Less texture                    More texture

## Patterns

Fabrics with patterns for both men and women tend to make an outfit more casual. A herringbone sport coat is more casual than a solid blazer. Large patterns used in main pieces or accessories make the outfit more casual. The mixture of patterns also makes the outfit more casual. For example, mixing a herringbone jacket with a cable sweater is more casual. Mixing tweed pants with a cable sweater set for women makes for a more casual look than if the pants are mixed with a solid-color silk blouse.

## Prints

Fabric with prints makes an outfit more casual. The size and the type of the print affect the level of dressiness of the outfit. Small geometrics create a more formal look. Medium to large abstract prints are more casual. Conversational prints featuring cartoons or "living" things such as animals and people, florals, etc., are more casual.

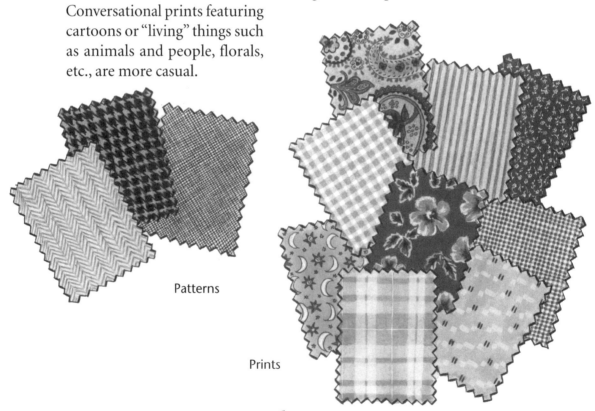

Patterns

Prints

# LAYERS

Using layers (more than one item on top) is an easy way to create business casual outfits. Layering changes the level of dressiness of an outfit. For example, a shirt with a vest and pants is dressier than a shirt alone with pants. A sweater set with a skirt or pants for women is dressier than a sweater alone with skirt or pants.

Layers: more than one item on top.

## CONSTRUCTION

Constructed silhouettes are those that make a garment stiff, such as a jacket with lining and creases. Constructed silhouettes make an outfit more dressy, unconstructed silhouettes make an outfit more casual. A tailored jacket is more dressy than a sweater. An unconstructed jacket or cardigan made of knitted wool is more casual than one made of worsted or gabardine wool which is stiff. If the outside of the garment or silhouette is softer and more flexible, it is more comfortable and gives a more relaxed look.

Constructed silhouettes: dressy          Unconstructed silhouettes: casual

# ACCESSORIES

The material, color, design, motif, and size of accessories affect the outfit, making it more dressy or more casual. Metals, gemstones, gold, and pearls are more formal. Leather, plastic, wood, hammered silver, make an outfit less formal. Ethnic motifs and large accessories are more casual. More accessories make an outfit more casual. The thickness of shoes also affects the level of dressiness of shoes. Thin-sole shoes are more dressy. Thicker-sole shoes make an outfit more casual.

**Accessories for Men**
Bold, geometric patterned ties
Smooth leather/ thicker sole
Tassel moccasin
Penny loafers

**Accessories for Women**
Ethnic motif necklace/earrings
Low heeled pump
Trouser shoe
Thicker rubber-sole shoes

## The Three Levels of Business Casual

Now that we know what makes an outfit more casual, we can choose just how casual we want to dress for a particular day. Since *one policy doesn't fit all*, we have defined three distinct levels of casual dressing to choose from. We've decided to call these different levels:

**Classic   Smart   Relaxed**

Following is a brief description of each level. In the next chapters, we include an extended list of items and more information on each level for women (Chapter 5) and for men (Chapter 6). The criteria for the selection of each level is described in Chapter 7.

---

**THE THREE LEVELS OF BUSINESS CASUAL**

**Classic Men - Key Item: Jacket**
Blazers and sport coats
Shirts and sweaters worn with a jacket
Wool, linen, silk-blend pants
Vests worn with a shirt and jacket

**Classic Women - Key Item: Jacket**
Pantsuits, matched or unmatched
Sweaters, worn with a jacket
Blouses and knit tops, worn with a jacket
Vests, worn with top and a jacket

**Smart Men - Key Item: Shirt with collar**
Shirts with collars and polo shirts
Mock, turtleneck, crew, V-neck, worn
   without a jacket
Bright colors, bold patterned ties, worn
   without a jacket
Khaki, linen, silk blends, corduroy pants

**Smart Women - Key Items: Two- or
   three-piece outfits or layers**
Wool, blends, or cotton pants
Short or long skirts
Sweaters and sweater sets
Blouses and knit tops with short or long
   sleeves

**Relaxed Men - Key Item: Jeans**
Jeans, denim, shorts
Shirts, with or without collars
Sweatshirt or T-shirt (no inappropriate mes-
   sages)
Sneakers (clean and in good condition)

**Relaxed Women - Key Items: Jeans,
   sleeveless tops**
Jeans, denim
Walking shorts
Short-sleeved and sleeveless blouses and tops
Sneakers (clean and in good condition)

## CLASSIC

This level also can be described as *formal business casual*. In the range of different levels of dressiness, the *Classic Level* is the closest to traditional business dress. The Classic Level begins where traditional tailored suits end. The starting point for this level is sport coats and blazers for men

**Men**
Blazers and sport coats
Colored and patterned shirts
Sweaters: mock, turtlenecks, crew, V-neck, *worn with a jacket*
Bolder designs, bright-colored ties
Wool, linen, silk-blend pants
Vests worn with a shirt and jacket
Thin- to medium-sole lace-up shoes or loafers

and pantsuits and separates with pants for women. The jacket is the key item that differentiates this level from other levels.

The message and perception that this type of clothing sends is that the wearer is professional, organized, reliable, consistent, and detail oriented.

**Women**
Pantsuits
Pants with a jacket
Sweaters: turtlenecks, crew, V-necks, *worn with a jacket*
Blouses and knit tops, *worn with a jacket*
Vests, *worn with top and a jacket*
Thin- to medium-sole shoes

## SMART

This level is probably one of the most widely accepted "interpretations" of business casual in many industries including manufacturing, high tech, health care, and education. This level features *two-piece outfits or layers without a jacket.* A more casual alternative to the tailored jacket/blazer for men is a casual cardigan sweater or vest with a shirt. A tie is optional. For women, a more relaxed alternative to the tailored jacket is a twin set or a blouse and a vest. The key elements of the *Smart Level* are two-piece out-

**Men**

Shirts with collars and polo shirts

Mock, turtlenecks, crew, V-neck, worn *without a jacket*

Bright colors, bold patterned ties, *worn without a jacket*

Khaki, linen, silk blends, corduroy pants

Vests worn with a shirt and jacket

Cardigan sweaters

Thin to medium leather or rubber sole shoes

fits or layers (without a jacket). Men's shirts must have a collar and women's tops must have sleeves.

The message and perception that this type of clothing conveys is creative, accessible, friendly, and competent.

## Women

Solid or patterned pants

Cotton pants ( khakis, twill, corduroys)

Short or long skirts

Lightweight, turtlenecks, crew, V-neck sweaters

Blouses and knit tops with short or long sleeves

Vests

Sweater sets

Cardigans and knit jackets

Unlined and unconstructed jackets— short, three-quarter, or long sleeves

Dresses in florals, knits, or jumpers

Flat leather pumps and trouser shoe with thin to medium soles

# RELAXED

Most companies approve of the first two business casual levels. The *Relaxed Level* is where many businesses draw the line. This level includes denim, jeans, T-shirts, and sneakers, clothing which is not appropriate for any other business casual level.

**Men**
Jeans
Cotton or knitted shirts, short or long sleeves
Shirts with or without collars
Polo-type shirts
Sweatshirt or T-shirt (no inappropriate messages)
Shorts
Denim jackets and vests
Sneakers (clean and in good condition)
Medium to thick leather or rubber sole shoes

The message and perception that this type of clothing sends out is creative, accessible, team player, and relaxed.

**Women**

Jeans

Skirts in denim, corduroy, leather, suede

Walking shorts

Blouses and knit tops

Short-sleeved and sleeve-less blouses and tops

Denim blouses, skirts, and jackets

T-shirts

Lightweight, turtlenecks, crew, V-neck sweaters

Sweater sets

Vests

Short-sleeved and sleeve-less dresses including florals, knits, and jumpers

Sneakers (clean and in good condition)

Medium- to thick-sole shoes

## Non-Appropriate Business Clothing

There are other types of clothing that are considered inappropriate for most business environments. These include weekend, beach, and exercise wear, such as jogging suits, exercise clothing, short shorts, halter tops, spandex, etc. There are some companies that will allow their employees who don't have direct contact with customers to wear this type of clothing. Other companies allow employees to wear these items for special days of the week or designated days during the year.

The fact is that these items and other articles of clothing from the *Relaxed Level*, such as jeans, sneakers, sleeveless tops, and others, are quite controversial. Most organizations that have established casual dress code policies are asking their employees to use discretion in selecting these pieces of clothing. To provide you with guidelines about these items, we conducted a survey of 165 top corporate executives around the country to tell us their opinion about the appropriateness of these controversial items. The results of the survey are presented in the next chapter.

# 4

# Appropriateness:
# Top Executives' Opinions

## The Survey

### Overview and Methodology

Because there are so many conflicting ideas of what is appropriate or inappropriate business casual attire, we decided to conduct a Business Casual survey to determine which of the more controversial articles of clothing were acceptable in business today.

- The survey was comprised of 165 male and female CEOs, VPs, and other top executives from medium and large corporations having at least 100 employees. It represented eight distinct business sectors in ten regions of the country. The survey was conducted via telephone and mail/fax in the winter of 1999.

- Respondents were asked to rate the controversial articles of clothing or accessories based on their own personal *opinions*. These opinions may have differed from their company policy or what actually happens in their office. Each item was rated as:

  - Unacceptable
  - Acceptable
  - Acceptable *only on designated days*

## Sectors Included in the Business Casual Survey

Travel & Hospitality
Finance (Banking, Insurance, Legal, Accounting)
Business Services (Consulting firms)
Real Estate, Realtors, Management companies
Public Administration (Federal/local government)
Public Relations, Advertising, Promotion
Utilities (Electric, Gas, Telephone, Water)
Health Care Management
Communications, Information Management (High Tech)

## Regions Included in the Survey

New York/Philadelphia Metro
New England
Washington, D.C., Metro
Mid-Western Region
South
Texas
Northern California
Southern California

## Company Size

Companies were classified by number of employees: 100–499, 500–999, and 1,000 or more. A review of results by these categories indicates that there is very little difference in opinions based on company size. The nationwide results are generally consistent regardless of how large or small a company is.

## Items of Clothing and Accessories Included in the Survey

### Items for Men and Women

- Denim shirts
- Denim pants
- T-shirts
- Sweatshirts and sweatpants
- Shorts
- Sneakers in general
- Tattoos
- Leather sandals with socks
- Denim jackets
- Jeans
- T-shirts with printed slogans
- Jogging suits
- Tennis sneakers
- No socks
- Leather sandals without socks
- Deck shoes

### Women only

- Leggings (tight stretch pants)
- Spandex (elastic, shiny tight pants for exercise)
- Wide-leg palazzo pants
- Sleeveless shirts, blouses, or tops
- Floral-print dresses
- Halter without a jacket (no sleeves and wrap around back of neck)
- Tube (sleeveless—no straps—tight around torso)
- Halter or Tube with a jacket
- Tank top without a jacket (low or medium cut—no sleeves)
- Tank top with a jacket
- Mini skirts
- Leather pants or skirts
- Walking shorts to the knee without a jacket
- Short shorts without a jacket
- Walking shorts with a jacket
- Skorts (shorts that have a piece of fabric in front and looks like skirt)
- Culottes (wide to-the-knee shorts)
- Long skirts to the ankle
- Open-toe leather sandals
- Slip-on buckled shoes
- See-through or bare midriff
- Thong or plastic sandals
- No hosiery (bare legs)

## NATIONWIDE RESULTS: MEN AND WOMEN

**Unacceptable by Wide Majority (more than 80%)**

- Jogging suits
- Sweatshirts and sweatpants
- Shorts
- T-shirts with printed slogans

**Unacceptable by Simple Majority (more than 51%)**

- No socks
- Tattoos
- Leather sandals without socks
- T-shirts
- Leather sandals with socks
- Tennis sneakers
- Sneakers in general
- Jeans

**Mixed Ratings** (similar percentages considered acceptable, unacceptable, and acceptable on designated days only)

- Denim pants
- Denim jackets
- Deck shoes
- Denim shirts

During the course of the survey, several respondents commented that *T-shirts with printed slogans* may be acceptable if the slogan refers to the corporate logo or products of the company.

A controversial discussion was that of tattoos. The general attitude is "if you have one, keep it covered."

## NATIONWIDE RESULTS: WOMEN ONLY

**Universally Unacceptable** (87% to 99%)

- See-though or bare midriff
- Spandex
- Short shorts without a jacket
- Tube top
- Halter without a jacket
- Tank top without a jacket
- Thong or plastic sandals

**Unacceptable by Wide Majority** (53% to 80%)

- Leggings
- Skirts with high slits
- Mini skirts
- Halter or tube with a jacket
- Walking shorts to the knee without a jacket
- Leather pants or skirts

**Mixed Ratings** (similar percentages considered acceptable, unacceptable, and acceptable on designated days only)

- Walking shorts with a jacket
- No hosiery
- Sleeveless shirts, blouses, or top
- Tank top with a jacket
- Open-toe leather sandals
- Skorts
- Wide-leg palazzo pants
- Culottes

**Acceptable in Most Offices**

- Long skirts to the ankle
- Floral-print dresses

## BUSINESS SECTOR RESULTS: MEN AND WOMEN

**Industries Consistent with National Results**

- Travel & Hospitality
- Finance
- Business Services
- Real Estate, Realtors, Management companies
- Public Administration
- Public Relations, Advertising, Promotion
- Health Care Management

**More Liberal Sectors** (compared to national results)

- Communications and Information Management (High Tech)
- Utilities and Natural Resources

**Communications and Information Management** (High Tech) accepts the following items significantly more than the national average:

- Tennis sneakers
- Sneakers in general
- Denim pants, jackets, and shirts

**Utilities and Natural Resources** accepts the following items slightly more than the national average:

- Denim jackets and shirts
- Deck shoes

## BUSINESS SECTOR RESULTS: WOMEN ONLY

### Consistent with National Results

• Travel & Hospitality
• Manufacturing and Distribution
• Business Services
• Real Estate, Realtors, Management companies
• Health Care Management

### More Conservative (compared to national results)

• Finance
• Public Administration

### More Liberal (compared to national results)

• Communications and Information Management (High Tech)
• Utilities and Natural Resources

**Communications and Information Management** were much more accepting of:

• Tank tops with a jacket
• Walking shorts with a jacket
• Sleeveless shirts
• Open-toe leather sandals
• No-hosiery
• Skorts
• Culottes
• Leggings
• Mini skirts
• Wide-leg palazzo pants

**Utilities and Natural Resources** were more accepting of:

• Culottes
• Open-toe leather sandals
• No hosiery

## RESULTS BY REGION: MEN AND WOMEN

**Consistent with National Results**
• Mid-Western Region
• Texas
• South

**More Liberal** (compared to national results)

• New England*
• Northern California
• Southern California

**New England** is more accepting of:
• No socks
• Leather sandals with or
   without socks
• Sneakers in general
• Tennis sneakers
• Tattoos

**Northern California** is more accepting of:
• No socks
• Sneakers in general
• Tennis sneakers
• Tattoos
• Jeans

**Southern California** is more accepting of:
• T-shirts

**Slightly More Conservative** (compared to national results)

• D.C. Metro
• New York/Philadelphia

**D.C. Metro** is less accepting of:
• Tattoos
• T-shirts
• Leather sandals
• Tennis sneakers
• Jeans

**New York/Philadelphia** is less accepting of:
• T-shirts with slogans
• Tennis sneakers

* Many respondents were from High-Tech companies

## RESULTS BY REGION: WOMEN ONLY

**Consistent with National Results**
• New York/Philadelphia Metro
• Mid-Western Region
• South

**More Liberal** (compared to national results)
• Southern California
• Northern California
• New England

**Southern California** is more accepting of:
• Walking shorts with a jacket
• Sleeveless shirts, blouses, or tops
• Tank top with a jacket
• Open-toe leather sandals

**Northern California** is more accepting of:
• Wide-leg palazzo pants
• Tank top with a jacket
• Skorts

**New England** is more accepting of:
• Wide-leg palazzo pants
• Open-toe leather sandals
• Skorts
• Walking shorts with a jacket
• Leather pants or skirts
• Floral-print dresses

**Washington, D.C., Metro** is *more conservative* compared to national results. It is less accepting of:
• Leggings
• No hosiery
• Sleeveless shirts, blouses, or tops
• Wide-leg palazzo pants
• Leather pants or skirts
• Floral-print dresses

## Recommendations

We believe that by providing you with this information, you will gain a perspective of what is considered appropriate and inappropriate in your industry.

If your organization has a written policy, this information can be used to supplement your current policy with the items that weren't addressed. You can use this as a guide to *"fill in the blanks"* and avoid items that are not mentioned in your organization's policy and that are considered inappropriate in your industry.

If you work in a company that doesn't have a written casual dress policy, this information will be a guide to those items that you should avoid.

# 5

# Business Casual Levels
# for Women

Classic also can be described as formal business casual. In the range of different levels of dressiness, the *Classic Level* is the closest to traditional business dress. Industries where employees dress more formally—such as banking, financial services, hospitality, and law firms—tend to select this level of casual for their employees' casual attire days. This level may also be the norm for many organizations that do not require formal business attire most work days.

The Classic Level begins where traditional tailored skirted suits end. The starting point is the pantsuit and separates with pants.

The jacket is the key item that differentiates the Classic Level from other levels. Layers created with sweaters, vests, or blouses worn with jackets are also options for this level.

### Items

| | |
|---|---|
| Pantsuits: | Constructed and unconstructed |
| Pants: | Wool, wool blends, silk blends, microfiber |
| Jackets: | Constructed and unconstructed |
| Skirts: | Short or long |
| Sweaters: | Lightweight, turtlenecks, crew, V-necks, worn with a jacket |
| Blouses/knit tops: | Worn with a jacket |
| Vests: | Worn with top and jacket |

## Combinations

Pantsuit with silk, cotton blouses

Pantsuit with knit top in cotton, silk, or cashmere; or
        sweater (turtleneck, crew, or V-neck)

Pants with silk, cotton blouses, and a jacket

Pants with knit top in cotton, silk, cashmere, and a jacket; or
        sweater (turtleneck, crew, or V-neck) and a jacket

Skirts with knit top in cotton, silk, cashmere, and a jacket; or
        sweaters (turtleneck, crew, V-neck) and a jacket

## Fabric

| | |
|---|---|
| Material: | Wool, wool blend, silk, rayon, microfiber |
| Texture: | Tightly woven fabrics that don't have much texture, such as wool, gabardine, silk, cotton |
| Color: | **Neutrals**-black, brown, gray, burgundy, taupe, camel<br>**Basics**- red, blue, green, teal, turquoise, olive, purple, rust, mahogany<br>**Lights and brights**- lavender, pink, yellow, coral, fuchsia, etc., for tops or scarves |
| Prints: | Small to medium prints not larger than the size of four quarters for blouses or vests |
| Pattern: | Small or subtle patterns, i.e., herringbone, tweeds, checks |

## Accessories

| | |
|---|---|
| Watch: | Gold or silver face with gold or metal band<br>gold or silver face with fine leather band |
| Pins/Necklaces: | Medium size in gold, silver, gemstones, such as ivory, onyx, or jade |
| Earrings: | Gold or silver in button style or square, round, or knot style |
| Shoes: | Shoe soles have thin to medium thickness, leather, either smooth or embossed; suede in a low or stacked heel; pumps with square or round toe |
| Socks/Hose: | Semi-sheer, opaque in color to match either hemline or shoe, trouser socks in solid colors that match either hemline or shoe |

## The Classic Level – Putting it all together

• Wear a jacket and keep all the items of clothing and accessories at the same level of dressiness.

•  Select tailored clothing with smooth fabrics that coordinate in color, fabric, and pattern.

## Appropriateness

Climate:          Slightly warm, cool to cold
Region:           Northwest, Midwest, and major metropolitan cities
Perceptions:   Professional, reliable, knowledgeable, efficient, trustworthy, conscientious, consistent, organized, and detail oriented

## Possible Benefits

*Supports you in:*
   • Positioning yourself as a leader
   • Portraying authority
   • Negotiating a deal
   • Obtaining a raise
   • Being considered for promotion

## Situations

This level of business casual is recommended for those situations in which you need to look more formal, more powerful, and authoritative.

It is recommended whenever you will make a presentation, lead a meeting with clients, visit a client who wears business casual attire, or meet someone for the first time where business casual dress is expected.

## SMART LEVEL FOR WOMEN

This level is probably one of the most widely accepted "interpretations" of business casual in most industries, including manufacturing, high tech, education, health care, pharmaceuticals, transportation, telecommunication, and so forth.

This level features *two-piece outfits or layers without a jacket.* A cardigan sweater, a knit, or unlined and unconstructed jacket are optional. The key elements of the *Smart Level* are two-piece outfits or layers (without a jacket).

**Items**

| | |
|---|---|
| Pants: | Wool, wool blends, silk blends, microfiber |
| Cotton pants: | Khaki, twill, corduroy |
| Skirts: | Short or long |
| Sweaters: | Lightweight, turtlenecks, crew, V-necks |

Vests
Blouses and knit tops
Sweater sets
Cardigans and knit jackets
Unlined and unconstructed jackets: short, three-quarter, or long sleeves
Unconstructed belted jackets
Dresses, including florals, knits, or jumpers
Walking shorts to the knee with blazer (if accepted by your organization)

# SMART LEVEL FOR WOMEN

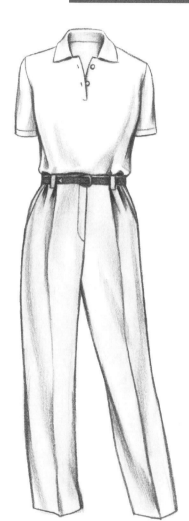

## SMART LEVEL FOR WOMEN

## SMART LEVEL FOR WOMEN

# SMART LEVEL FOR WOMEN

## Combinations

Pants with blouse
Pants with blouse and cardigan
Pants with blouse and vest
Pants with cotton knit top or sweater: turtleneck, crew, and V-neck
Pants with cotton knit top or sweater: turtleneck, crew, and vest
Pants with sweater set

Cotton pants (khaki, twill, corduroy) with blouse
Cotton pants (khaki, twill, corduroy) with blouse and cardigan
Cotton pants (khaki, twill, corduroy) with blouse and vest
Cotton pants (khaki, twill, corduroy) with cotton knit top or sweater:
            turtleneck, crew, and V-neck
Cotton pants (khaki, twill, corduroy) with cotton knit top or sweater:
            turtleneck, crew, and vest
Cotton pants (khaki, twill, corduroy) with sweater set

Skirt with blouse
Skirt with blouse and cardigan
Skirt with blouse and vest
Skirt with cotton knit top or sweater: turtleneck, crew, and V-neck
Skirt with cotton knit top or sweater: turtleneck, crew, and vest
Skirt with sweater set

Jumper with blouse
Jumper with cotton knit top or sweater: turtleneck, crew, and V-neck

Unconstructed jacket with blouse, knit top, and pants
Belted jacket with blouse, knit top, and pants

Dress with sweater

Walking shorts to the knee with blazer (if accepted by your organization)

## Fabric

| | |
|---|---|
| Material: | Wool, wool blend, linen blends, cotton, cotton blend, i.e., with lycra, silk, rayon, twill, corduroy, and microfiber |
| Texture: | Light, medium to heavy weight, loosely woven fabrics that have some texture, such as wool crepe, wool flannel, twill, linen blends, raw silk, corduroy |
| Color: | **Neutrals**-navy, black, brown, gray, burgundy, taupe, camel<br>**Basics**-red, blues, green, teal, turquoise, olive, purple<br>**Lights and brights**-lavender, pink, orange, violet, coral, fuchsia, etc., turquoises, combined with neutral colors, light and bright colors for main pieces |
| Prints: | Plaids, dots, florals, stripes, checks, geometrics, abstracts, conversational prints, not larger than the size of four quarters |
| Pattern: | Medium to large patterns, such as bold plaids, wide window pane |

## Accessories

| | |
|---|---|
| Watch: | Gold or silver face and band<br>gold or silver face with leather band |
| Pins/Necklaces: | Medium size in matte finish gold, silver, or craft type design, ceramic, beads, ethnic motifs |
| Earrings: | Gold, silver, or matte finish in hoop, short dangling, or drop style |
| Shoes: | Soles range from thin to thick leather, either smooth or embossed suede in a flat, low stacked or platform heels, moccasins, trouser shoes, loafers |
| Socks/Hose: | Trouser socks in a solid or pattern, opaque hose, color to match either hemline or shoe |

## The Smart Level – Putting it all together

- Coordinate clothing and accessories comparable in texture, construction, and color.

- Use two- or three-piece outfits or layers.

- Use cardigan sweaters and jackets only if they are loose and belted for a more casual look.

## Appropriateness

Climate:        Slightly warm, cool to cold
Region:         Any location in the United States
Perceptions:    Creative, accessible, friendly, competent, dependable, original

## Possible Benefits

*Supports you in:*
- Being a team player
- Building relationships with clients and co-workers
- Creating an informal working atmosphere

## Situations

This level of business casual is recommended for most situations that require an informal atmosphere and relaxed environment. It is appropriate for internal meetings if other attendees are also wearing business casual attire.

This level is also appropriate for most conferences and training sessions that call for business casual attire. You may want to keep a jacket on hand in case a situation arises requiring more formality.

## RELAXED LEVEL FOR WOMEN

This is the level where companies and employees draw the line. The addition of denim and jeans are the key elements of this level. Some companies consider denim and jeans as appropriate business casual attire while other companies make it clear to their employees that jeans are not accepted as part of their business casual dress policy.

This level also includes T-shirts, sneakers,  shorts and sandals that are not appropriate for any other levels.

### Items

Jeans
Shorts
Skirts: denim, corduroy, leather, suede, challis, short or long and full
Walking shorts
Blouses and knit tops
Short-sleeved and sleeveless blouses and tops
Denim blouses, skirts and jackets
T-shirts
Sweaters: lightweight, turtlenecks, crew, V-necks
Sweater sets
Vests
Short-sleeved and sleeveless dresses, including florals, knits, and jumpers

# RELAXED LEVEL FOR WOMEN

# RELAXED LEVEL FOR WOMEN

* If permitted by your organization

### Combinations

Cotton pants (khaki, twill, corduroy) with T-shirt

Jeans with blouse
Jeans with blouse and cardigan
Jeans with blouse and vest
Jeans with cotton knit top or sweater: turtleneck, crew, and V-neck
Jeans with cotton knit top or sweater: turtleneck, crew, and vest
Jeans with sweater set
Jeans with T-shirt
Jeans with denim top or jacket

Denim skirt with blouse
Denim skirt with blouse and cardigan
Denim skirt with blouse and vest
Denim skirt with cotton knit top or sweater: turtleneck, crew, and V-neck
Denim skirt with cotton knit top or sweater: turtleneck, crew, and vest
Denim skirt with sweater set
Denim skirt with T-shirt
Denim skirt with denim top or jacket
Denim jumper with blouse
Denim jumper with cotton knit top or sweater: turtleneck, crew, and V-neck

Walking shorts* at the knee with knit cotton, crew, or V-neck top
Walking shorts at the knee with short-sleeved blouse
Walking shorts at the knee with short-sleeved blouse and cardigan
Walking shorts at the knee with short- or long-sleeved blouse and vest
Walking shorts at the knee with sweater set
Walking shorts at the knee with T-shirt
Walking shorts at the knee with denim top or jacket

*If permitted by your organization

## Fabric

| | |
|---|---|
| Material: | Cotton, denim, corduroy, chambray |
| Texture: | Light, medium to heavy weight, maximum texture, crisp and coarse fabrics like denim |
| Color: | **Neutrals**-navy, black, brown, gray, burgundy, taupe, camel |
| | **Basics**-red, blues, green, teal, turquoise, olive, purple lights and brights—lavender, pink, orange, violet, coral, fuchsia, turquoise, etc., combined with neutral colors |
| | **Light and bright colors**-for main pieces, tops, and accessories |
| Prints: | Plaids, florals, checks, geometrics, stripes, abstracts, dots, conversational prints, combination of different patterns and prints |
| Pattern: | Medium to large patterns |

## Accessories

| | |
|---|---|
| Watch: | Gold or silver face with leather or plastic bands, sport or decorative watches in varied colors |
| Pins/Necklaces: | Medium size in gold, silver, or craft type design, ceramic, beads, ethnic motifs |
| Earrings: | Gold, silver, or matte finish stone in hoop, short dangling, or drop style |
| Shoes: | Shoe soles range from medium to thick leather, either smooth or embossed; suede in a low stacked or platform heel, moccasins, trouser shoes, loafers Sneakers: clean and in good condition Low to medium heel sandals |
| Socks/Hose: | Trouser socks in a solid or pattern, opaque hose color to match either hemline or shoe |

## The Relaxed Level – Putting it all together

• Clothing must be clean, wrinkle, and stain free.
• Clothing should not be too tight, short, revealing, or too baggy.
• T-shirts are acceptable only without inappropriate messages.

## Appropriateness

Climate:       Slightly warm, cool to cold
Region:        Warm-weather states, summertime around the United
               States, any location in the United States
Perceptions:   Creative, accessible, friendly, relaxed, easy going,
               innovative

## Possible Benefits

*Supports you in:*
• Being a team player
• Building relationships with co-workers
• Fostering a friendly and relaxed working atmosphere

## Situations

This level of business casual is recommended only for those organizations that have clearly defined that jeans, T-shirts, and denim are appropriate.

This level fosters the most informal and relaxed work environment. It is appropriate when working by yourself and not meeting with clients or the public, or when working on team projects that require creativity and informality. It is also appropriate for very casual training sessions and off-site retreats.

**SMART**

Key Items= Two-piece outfits or layers

Pants/skirt with blouse / knit top or vest

Pants/skirt with sweater set

**CLASSIC**

Key Item = Jacket

Pantsuit with blouse or knit top

Pants with blouse or knit top and jacket

**RELAXED**

Key Items = Jeans/sleeveless tops

Jeans - cotton pants

Denim - skirts /tops

T- shirts

Sneakers - sandals

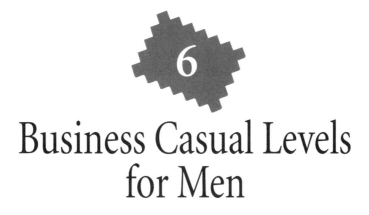

# Business Casual Levels for Men

Classic also can be described as formal business casual. In the range of different levels of dressiness or formality, the *Classic Level* is the closest to traditional business dress. The industries that tend to select this level of dress for their employees' casual attire days are those where employees dress more formally, such as in banking, financial services, hospitality, and law firms. This level may also be the norm for many organizations that do not require formal business attire most workdays.

The Classic Level begins where tailored suits end, and moves men on the fashion continuum from suits to blazers and sport coats, with ties as an optional item.

The starting point of this level is the jacket, an essential item that differentiates the Classic Level from the others. A jacket can be worn with or without a tie. Layers created with sweaters or vests are also options for this level.

## Items

Tailored blazers

Tailored sport coats

Shirts:          Solid colored, striped, and other patterns

Sweaters:     Lightweight mock, turtlenecks, crew,
                    V-neck—*worn with a shirt and jacket*

Ties:            Bright colors, bold patterns
                    woven/knit/silk/wool

Pants:          Wool, linen, silk blends
                    cuffed or uncuffed

Vests:          *Worn with a shirt and jacket*

## Combinations

Blazer/sport coat with button-down shirts, tie or no tie

Blazer/sport coat with light or colored striped shirts, tie or no tie

Blazer/sport coat with knit polo sweater

Blazer/sport coat with shirt and knit sweater

Blazer/sport coat with turtleneck or mock turtleneck sweaters

Blazer/sport coat with vest, shirt, tie or no tie

# CLASSIC LEVEL FOR MEN

## CLASSIC LEVEL FOR MEN

## Blazers

Navy

Forest, olive

Gray

Camel

## Sport Coats

Herringbone

Tweed

Windowpane

Linen-silk blends

Houndstooth

Glen plaid

Bold patterns

## Details

Single or double breasted

Top stitching

No leather patches

Metal, plastic, or leather buttons

Pockets or flaps

## Shirts *(long or short sleeves)*

### *Patterns/style*

Solids—light colors

Solids—medium to dark colors

Bolder stripes

Oxford button-down

Plaids

Turtleneck

V-neck

Crew neck

Woven prints

### *Fabrics*

Broadcloth

Microfiber

Oxford

Tattersall

Linen

Knits

Silk

Rayon

## Pants

Light- to medium-weight wools

Wool/linen blends

Flannels

Cuffed or non-cuffed

Houndstooth checks

Wool/silk blends

Pleated

## Sweaters

Cashmere
Fine cotton
Turtleneck

Wool
Crew neck

## Vests

Wool
Linen/rayon

Linen
Knits

## Ties

*Patterns/style*
Stripes—fine or bold
Paisley
Club
Medallion
Abstract
Florals
Hand painted
Conversational prints

*Fabric*
Silk
Wool
Cotton knits
Matte finish—woven

## Other Accessories

*Shoes:* *Thin to medium soles*
Lace-up oxfords
Wing-tip oxford
Tasseled loafer
Loafers with buckles
Suede leather oxfords
Leather monk strap

*Socks:*
Dark color socks
Discreet patterns
Argyles in dark colors

*Braces:*
Solid colors
Patterns

*Belts:*
Embossed or smooth leather belts
Calfskin
Reptile skin type

*Watch:*
Gold or silver face and band
Gold or silver face with either fine
    leather or metal band

## The Classic Level – Putting it all together

- Wear a jacket and keep all the items of clothing and accessories at the same level of dressiness.
- Keep tie patterns not larger than the size of three quarters.
- Select tailored clothing with smooth fabrics that coordinate in color, fabric, and pattern.
- Shoes must have thin soles and shouldn't be too formal, i.e., wing tips.

## Appropriateness

Climate:       Slightly warm, cool to cold
Region:        Northeast, Midwest, and major metropolitan cities
Perceptions:   Professional, reliable, conscientious, consistent, depend-
               able, organized, and detail oriented

## Possible Benefits

*Supports you in:*
- Positioning yourself as a leader
- Portraying authority
- Negotiating a deal
- Obtaining a raise
- Being considered for promotion

## Situations

This level of business casual is recommended for those situations in which you need to look more formal, more powerful, and authoritative.

It is recommended whenever you will make a presentation, lead a meeting with clients, visit a client who wears business casual attire, or meet someone for the first time where business casual dress is expected.

## SMART LEVEL FOR MEN

This level is probably one of the most widely accepted "interpretations" of business casual in most industries, including manufacturing, high tech, education, health care, pharmaceuticals, transportation, telecommunications, and so forth.

This level features *two-piece outfits or layers without a jacket.* Tie is optional. Layers can be created with shirts worn with vests and sweaters. Another option for layers is a T-shirt in medium or dark colors worn underneath a collared shirt. The white T-shirt is too casual for this level although is acceptable in the Relaxed Level. The key item for this level is the *collared shirt.*

### Items

| | |
|---|---|
| Shirts: | Long or short sleeved with collar, solid colored, striped, and other patterns |
| | Polo type |
| Sweaters: | Lightweight mock, turtlenecks, cardigan, crew, V-neck-*worn without a jacket* |
| Ties: | Bright colors, bold patterns—*worn without a jacket* woven/knit/cotton |
| Pants: | Khaki, wool, linen, silk blends, corduroy, twill Cuffed or uncuffed |
| Vests: | Worn with a shirt |

### Combinations

Pants with shirt, tie or no tie
Pants with shirt, knit sweater, tie or no tie
Pants with shirt, vest, tie or no tie
Pants with shirt, cardigan sweater
Pants with collared shirt and T-shirt in a color (not white) underneath

# SMART LEVEL FOR MEN

# SMART LEVEL FOR MEN

# SMART LEVEL FOR MEN

**Pants**

| | |
|---|---|
| Khaki | Chinos |
| Twill | Houndstooth checks |
| Corduroy | Pleated flannels |
| Wool/silk blends | Cuffed or non-cuffed |
| Wool/linen blends | Light- to medium-weight wools |

**Shirts** *(With collars)*

| | |
|---|---|
| Long, or short sleeved dress shirts | Long, or short sleeved sport shirts |
| Banded collar | Polo shirts |
| Solids, light colors | Broadcloth |
| Solids, medium to dark colors | Cotton madras |
| Bolder stripes | Rayon |
| Oxford button-down | Tattersall |
| Plaids | Linen |
| Woven prints | Knits |
| Bolder patterns | Silk |

**Sweaters**

| | |
|---|---|
| Turtleneck/mock turtleneck | Pullovers |
| V-neck | Crew neck |
| Cardigan | Vest |

**Other Accessories**

| | |
|---|---|
| *Braces:* | Solid bright colors |
| | Patterns |
| *Watch:* | Gold or silver face with metal or leather bands |
| *Shoes:* | *Thin to medium leather or rubber soles* |
| | Leather loafers |
| | Penny loafers |
| | Loafers with buckles |
| | Suede leather oxfords |
| | Rubber-sole shoes |
| | Monk strap in leather or suede |
| *Socks:* | Colored socks |
| | Bold patterns |
| | Argyles |
| *Belts:* | Reptile skin-type belts |
| | Embossed leather belts |
| | Calfskin |

## The Smart Level – Putting it all together

• Coordinate clothing and accessories with comparable texture and color.
• Use layers to move from more casual to less casual.
• Use vests and cardigan sweaters with or without a tie.
• Keep shirt prints not larger than the size of three quarters.
• Wear shirt and tie without a jacket.
• All shirts must have a collar.
• Shirts can be dress shirts or sport shirts.
• T-shirts in color other than white worn underneath collared shirts.

## Appropriateness

Climate:  Slightly warm, cool to cold
Region:    Any location in the United States
Perceptions:   Creative, accessible, friendly, competent, dependable,
                original

## Possible benefits

*Supports you in:*
• Being a team player
• Building relationships with clients and co-workers
• Creating an informal working atmosphere

## Situations

This level of business casual is recommended for most situations that require an informal atmosphere and relaxed environment. It is appropriate for internal meetings if other attendees are also wearing business casual attire.

This level is also appropriate for most conferences and training sessions that call for business casual attire. You may want to keep a blazer on hand in case the situation arises requiring more formality.

## RELAXED CASUAL FOR MEN

This is the level where companies draw the line. The addition of *denim and jeans* are the key elements of this level. Some companies consider denim and jeans as appropriate business casual attire, while other companies make it clear that jeans and shorts are not acceptable as part of their business casual dress policy. This level also includes T-shirts and sneakers, which are not appropriate for any other business casual level.

### Items

| | |
|---|---|
| Jeans | Khakis |
| Cotton or corduroy pants | Polo-type shirts |
| Shorts | |

Cotton or knitted shirts, short or long sleeves
Collared, collarless or banded collar shirts
Sweatshirt or T-shirt (no inappropriate messages)
Denim jackets and vests
Wool or cotton ties with jeans and corduroys
Sneakers, clean and in good condition

### Combinations

Jeans with printed or solid shirt
Jeans with woven or polo shirt
Jeans with T-shirt or sweater
Jeans with wool, silk, or corduroy blazer
Jeans with denim jacket
Cotton or corduroy pants with shirt or sweater
Khakis with denim shirt or jacket
Khakis with T-shirt
Khakis with knit shirt without collar
Pants with white T-shirt underneath shirt or sweater
Shorts with solid or printed shirt, polo shirt or T-shirt

# RELAXED CASUAL FOR MEN

*If permitted by your organization

# RELAXED CASUAL FOR MEN

*If permitted by your organization

## Pants

| | |
|---|---|
| Jeans | Khaki |
| Corduroy | Cotton |

## Shirts *(with or without collars)*

| | |
|---|---|
| T-shirts | Knits |
| Polo shirts | Woven prints |
| Oxford button-down | Bolder stripes |
| Solids—light colors | Solids—medium to dark colors |
| Tattersall | Plaids |
| Cotton madras | Bolder patterns |
| Broadcloth | Rayon |
| Linen | Silk |

## Sweaters *(worn with jeans or corduroys)*

| | |
|---|---|
| Turtleneck | Pullover |
| V-neck | Crew neck |
| Cardigan | |

## Other Accessories

*Shoes:* Medium to thick leather or rubber soles
Penny loafers
Suede or leather monk straps
Fisherman's sandals
Sneakers

*Belts:* Woven leather belts
Canvas belts

*Socks:* Colored socks
Bold patterns
Argyles

*Watch:* Gold or silver face with leather or plastic bands, i.e.
sport, tank, nautical-type watches

## The Relaxed Level – Putting it all together

• Clothing must be clean, wrinkle, and stain-free.
• Clothing should not be too tight or too baggy.
• T-shirts should not carry inappropriate messages.

## Appropriateness

Climate:        Slightly warm, cool to cold
Region:         Summertime, any location in the United States; all-year warm weather states
Perceptions:   Creative, accessible, friendly, relaxed, easy going, innovative

## Possible Benefits

*Supports you in:*
• Being a team player
• Building relationships with co-workers
• Creating an informal and friendly working atmosphere

## Situations

This level of business casual is recommended only for those organizations that have clearly defined that jeans, T-shirts, and denim are appropriate.

This level fosters the most informal and relaxed work environment. It is appropriate when working by yourself and not meeting with clients or the public, or when working on team projects that require creativity and informality. It is also appropriate for very casual training sessions and off-site retreats.

**CLASSIC**
Key Item = Jacket
Jacket, shirt, and tie
Jacket, shirt, no tie

**SMART**
Key Item = Shirt with collar
Polo or knit shirt with collar
Tie optional, no jacket

**RELAXED**
Key Item = Jeans
Jeans, denim
T-shirt, shirt without collar
Sneakers

# Criteria for Selecting the Appropriate Business Casual Level

## Which Level — When and Why?

This chapter will assist you at that *critical time in the morning when you get ready to face the world.* During this hour when you plan your workday, your agenda will dictate the types of activities scheduled, the people you will interact with, the skills that you need to exercise, and the clothes you will wear.

There are many variables to consider when answering the simple question: *What do I wear?* There isn't just one single standard for dressing appropriately anymore. The golden rule of dressing for business today is to apply *audience analysis* and to consider what your image objective is. This means, determine who you will be dealing with so that what you are wearing matches the people and the situation. Our clothes send a message whether we want them to or not.

There are still many business situations that will require traditional business attire. For example, if you are in sales or are attending a meeting overseas, a board meeting, or negotiating money, traditional business attire will be your best choice.

If casual dress is an option, the appropriate attire depends on many variables, such as your profession, job profile, position in the organization, corporate culture, where you are located, the specific business occasion, type of interactions, and the message you want your image to convey.

## The Questions

The following are some of the questions you need to ask yourself.

### Questions about YOU

What is your job and position in the company? _____

What is the company's dress code and culture? _____

Which sector do you work in? _____

What is the standard of dress in your industry? _____

### Questions about your AGENDA

What are your responsibilities for the day? _____

Who are you meeting? _____

Where is the meeting? _____

What do you want to achieve? _____

What message do you want to convey? _____

### Questions about your AUDIENCE

What will your client be wearing? _____

What will your supervisor be wearing? _____

What will your colleagues be wearing? _____

## The Answers

What you wear depends largely on your position/job, where you work, and what kind of business you are in. Specific industries, jobs, and geography all dictate their own clothing standards. To determine the appropriate level of business casual dress and the items in that level, you need to consider the following variables:

- Industry
- Organization culture
- Position/job
- Location
- Activities/interactions
- Desired perception

### Industry

The first rule of effective dressing is common sense. While a Wall Street broker might wear a two-piece suit and not even consider wearing business casual at all, an advertising executive may need to wear something to demonstrate creativity. People who work in the financial industry tend to dress more conservatively. When money is involved, customers prefer traditional clothing that conveys stable and conservative values. People who work in high tech, real estate, communications, and information management are allowed the freedom to dress more casually. In advertising, entertainment, and other cutting-edge industries, it is important to show that you are up-to-date on the latest trends.

When selecting the appropriate Business Casual Level, you will find that "casual days" at a law firm may call for Classic with the key item being a jacket for both men and women. For an advertising agency, the Relaxed Level, with pressed jeans and a colored shirt, may be appropriate for the creative department, and so on.

Below are some general guidelines to help determine the degree of formality of some industries and the level of business casual that will be most appropriate.

| Type of Business | Recommended Business Casual Level |
|---|---|
| **Conservative Industries**<br>Banking<br>Insurance<br>Legal/Accounting<br>Business Services/Consulting firms<br>Hospitality (property level) | Classic Level and Smart Level if accepted by organization |
| **Semi-Conservative**<br>Travel & Hospitality<br>Real Estate, Management Companies<br>Public Administration:<br>    Federal/local government<br>Public Relations—Advertising<br>Association Management | Smart Level and Relaxed Level if accepted by organization |
| **Semi-Conservative and Informal**<br>Utilities (Electric, Gas, Telephone, Water)<br>Health Care Management<br>Communications and Information<br>    Management<br>High Tech<br>Manufacturing<br>Education | Smart Level and Relaxed Level if accepted by organization |

*Note:* Regardless of your industry, if you are meeting a client for the first time, or are dealing with customers, you may want to choose the Classic Level. Choose the other levels—Smart and Relaxed—according to your industry and for those *no client contact* days.

## Organization Culture

Within your sector, there are other considerations to keep in mind when selecting your business casual attire. Is your organization's culture open and relaxed? Does your organization have clear, written dress code policies? Is the dress code in your organization written or verbal? If your organization has a written policy, following the guidelines will help you choose the appropriate level. If your organization has a casual dress policy in which some items of clothing are considered inappropriate, this will make the selection easy. For example, if your organization doesn't approve of jeans and T-shirts, the Classic or the Smart Levels will be your only choices. If your organization prefers that you wear jackets with your business casual attire, especially when you meet with clients, the Classic Level will be the dress code to follow.

**Organizations with Dress Code Policies**-Read the policy carefully and determine which levels fit into the policy. Most companies' policies match our Classic and Smart Levels. If your organization allows jeans and T-shirts, then you can include the Relaxed Level as a third option.

Observe those employees that are involved in defining written dress code policies. They understand exactly what management wants to see as the appropriate business casual dress and what they consider inappropriate. These people have the responsibility of being a role model to others. Follow their lead.

**Organizations without a Dress Code Policy**-If there is no written policy, you need to interpret the unwritten policy. Observation and common sense will be your best guidelines. Look around the company for standards. Observe your superiors and respected peers. Look at what the successful men and women are wearing and try to emulate them. Chances are they are doing something right.

## Location

Geographic differences are also important. Where are you doing business? West Coast? East Coast? Midwest? Metropolitan area? Small city? Small town? Rural or urban area? A style that looks right in Chicago might seem stuffy in San Francisco or too provincial in Dallas. Black and neutral colors are appropriate in most cities. A style that is appropriate in some areas will be inappropriate in others. Fashions become more casual the farther West one travels. Less formal casual attire is more accepted in the West, in warm weather locations, and across the country during the summertime when most companies relax their dress codes.

## Position/Job

Your type of job and responsibilities will guide you in selecting the right attire for business. Are you a manager? Do you supervise a team? Do you have many employees under your supervision? Or are you a team member without any supervisory responsibilities? Does your job have high visibility? Does your job have high contact with clients? Are you often representing your organization outside the office? Are you in sales or marketing? Or are you in a technical position with minimal or no client contact?

If your job has high visibility and you have management responsibilities, choose Classic or Smart depending on the situation and the perception you want to convey. If your position requires supervision of many employees, remember that you will be a role model for your team, therefore you need to clarify what type of business casual you want them to wear because they will follow your example.

If your job doesn't require supervisory responsibilities and has low visibility with low or no client contact, choose Smart or Relaxed Levels depending on your organization's dress policy.

Remember that when dealing with clients, as we will discuss next, the client contact will dictate your choice of attire.

As a supervisor there will be times you don't want to dress too casually. You might want to wear Classic in situations in which you want to demonstrate some authority and Smart when you want to be seen as one of the team.

### Activities /Interactions

In our customer service-based society, most business rules are dictated by the client's expectations. Our clients determine not only how we perform, but how we dress. The activities and interactions scheduled for the day will help you to choose the appropriate business casual attire.

What is the meeting about? Why are you having the meeting? What is the purpose of the meeting? Are you trying to get someone's business or are you trying to solve a problem? Do you need to set people at ease or impress them? Are you the buyer or the seller? Are you going over routine matters or into new and serious negotiations? If it is an established relationship, what you wear is not as critical as if this is a new relationship.

**Meeting with Clients** - "I dress primarily for the customer—what the customer is used to. Which look do they prefer? If I don't know, I would ask," claim many executives who want to be sure they are appropriately dressed. If meeting with potential clients, choose Traditional Business attire, Classic, or, if they dress casually, Smart. For a casual look, choose between the Classic and the Smart Levels depending on your organization's accepted guidelines and the client's preferences. If checking in with long-time customers and you want to make them feel comfortable, the Smart will always be appropriate. When visiting clients outside your office, ask about their appropriate dress code and dress accordingly. The golden rule is to learn to coordinate the dress policy between you and your client.

**Internal Meetings**- For meetings with your supervisor, follow his or her lead. Don't dress better or at a much lower level of formality than the person you want to build rapport with. If you want to put someone at ease, choose the Smart or Relaxed Levels depending on your organization's dress code.

A common rule for business is to dress in standard traditional business attire for important meetings with outside business people. They still expect to see a business suit or a jacket when a business deal is closed. Suits are still needed for a business trip to most countries overseas.

If you are meeting with internal customers from other departments, treat them as customers and follow their attire. If you want to put them at ease, choose the Smart or Relaxed Level if appropriate in your organization. If you are making a presentation or are negotiating, wear the Classic or Smart Level. A jacket will always add credibility to your presentation and can be removed for a less dressy look.

## Activities

Specific job activities demand different looks. Delivering a presentation to a client may require your traditional power business look or the Classic Level. Leading a planning session with your team may require your Relaxed look.

Are you presenting a budget or a new program for approval? Are you negotiating? The Classic look will provide you with added credibility and respect.

Are you having a planning meeting where creativity and exchange of ideas is critical? The Relaxed or Smart Levels will promote a flexible, creative atmosphere.

Is this a regular day at the office without client contact? Will you be working with equipment, machinery, and not much human contact? Will you be cleaning up files, organizing your desk, or making phone calls without any critical meeting? Depending on your organization's culture, the Smart or Relaxed Levels will provide you with the comfort you need to be productive. Keep a jacket on hand in your office in case you are called to an unexpected meeting.

---

**Summary**

- Internal meetings where you will be leading or presenting—Wear a traditional business look or Classic Level.

- Internal meetings or routine tasks without additional internal or external customers—Select Smart or Relaxed depending on which is accepted in your organization.

- External meetings representing your organization—Wear a traditional business look unless explicitly advised that business casual is acceptable. If business casual is expected, choose Classic or Smart depending on the client's guidelines.

---

## Messages/Desired Perception

Your clothes send visual messages and create perceptions. What is your purpose for the day? Are you trying to get someone's business or are you trying to be persuasive? Do you need to put clients or co-workers at ease or impress them? Are you expected to be highly visible today? Will you be representing your company to outside people? Do you want to build rapport? Do you expect to be counted as a part of the team?

When you want to exercise power, authority, and credibility, the Classic Level will provide you with the positive visual image to achieve this goal. This level, which includes the jacket, will support you in creating these perceptions: being credible, authoritative, solid, competent, centered, dependable, organized, trustworthy, honest, educated, analytical, precise, friendly, technical, expressive, professional, logical.

If you want to build rapport, put people at ease, and foster communication, the Smart and the Relaxed Levels will be the appropriate choices. The Smart Level will help you to be perceived as creative, flexible, accommodating, cutting-edge artistic, dependable, creative, original, friendly, expressive. By selecting the Relaxed Level, you will be perceived as creative, flexible, cutting edge , artistic, fun-loving, warm, original, friendly, expressive.

## Other Tips

When unsure, ask. With different standards of dress today, no one will be surprised or offended by the question. It is important to ask what is the appropriate dress in the client's organization and what will be the appropriate attire for a specific meeting. Your client will appreciate that you care enough to make the inquiry.

# Summary of Appropriate Levels of Business Casual and Selection Criteria

When selecting your clothes, take into consideration:

**Your JOB/POSITION**
- Daily responsibilities
- Interactions with:
    colleagues
    team members
    clients
    consultants

**Your AGENDA**
- Responsibilities for the day
- Meetings:
    attendees
    location: in or out of office
    goals/desired perception

**Your AUDIENCE**
- Colleagues: how they dress
- Supervisor: how he/she dresses
- Clients: new or existing
    how they dress

**Desired PERCEPTION**
- Powerful/authoritative
- Credible/respectful
- Professional/efficient
- Knowledgeable/organized
- Accessible/friendly
- Creative/original

Always keep a jacket at hand... for unexpected situations that may require more formality!

Since the Traditional Business Attire is still appropriate and expected for many business situations, the following page summarizes when to choose it.

# Traditional Business Attire

## Perceptions

Most authoritative, credible, respectful, professional, solid, analytical, precise, dominant, logical, reliable

## Possible Benefits

*Supports you in:*
- Positioning yourself as a leader, as an authority figure, as an expert
- Negotiating a deal
- Leading groups and meetings

## Situations

- When you need to look most powerful, most formal,
- When you need to match your client's formality

## It is appropriate for

- Representing your company outside the organization
- Meeting clients for the first time
- Making a presentation
- Leading a meeting with clients
- Visiting a client who wears traditional business attire
- Doing business internationally

## CLASSIC LEVEL

**Select the Classic Level** when:

- Your organization's culture seems to be **formal or semi-formal**
- You desire to be perceived as **reliable/organized, consistent/precise**
- You work in the following **industries** listed on this chart
- You have any of the listed **positions/jobs**
- You will be having any of the listed **interactions**

| Industry | Position/Job | Interactions |
|---|---|---|
| Banking | Upper mgt. | Clients: external*** |
| Insurance | Middle mgt. | Clients: internal |
| Legal/Accounting | Professional | Meetings: external*** |
| Business Services | Technical | Meetings: internal |
| Consulting Firms | Contractor | Presentations |
| Travel & Hospitality | Consultant | Representing company*** |
| Public Administration* | Sales-marketing | Negotiations |
| Health Care Management | Customer service rep | Conventions |
| Utilities** | Instructor | |
| Communications | Receptionist | |
| High Tech | | |
| Education | | |

* Federal and local government
** Electric, Gas, Telephone, Water
***When business casual is the expected attire

# SMART LEVEL

## Select the Smart Level when:

- Your organization's culture seems to be **semi-formal** or **somewhat conservative**
- You desire to be perceived as **friendly/creative, approachable/original**
- You work in the following **industries** listed on this chart
- You have any of the listed **positions/jobs**
- You will be having any of the listed **interactions**

| Industry | Position/Job | Interactions |
|---|---|---|
| Banking | Upper mgt. | Clients: external* |
| Insurance | Middle mgt. | Clients: internal |
| Legal/Accounting | Professional | Meetings: external |
| Business Services | Technical | Meetings: internal |
| Consulting Firms | Support | Social gatherings* |
| Travel & Hospitality | Contractor | Representing company* |
| Public Administration** | Consultant | Off-site retreats |
| Health Care Management | Sales/marketing | Conventions* |
| Utilities*** | Customer service rep | |
| Communications | | |
| High Tech | | |
| Education | | |
| Manufacturing | | |

\* When business casual is the expected attire

\** Federal and local government

\*** Electric, Gas, Telephone, Water

## RELAXED LEVEL

**Select the Relaxed Level** when:

- Your organization's culture seems to be **informal**
- You desire to be perceived as **friendly/creative, easy going, original/expressive**
- You work in the following **industries** listed on this chart
- You have any of the listed **positions/jobs**
- You will be having any of the listed **interactions**

| **Industry** | **Position/Job** | **Interactions** |
|---|---|---|
| Banking | Middle mgt. | Clients: internal |
| Insurance | Professional | Meetings: internal* |
| Legal/Accounting | Technical | Off-site retreats |
| Business Services | Contractor | |
| Consulting Firms | Support | |
| Travel & Hospitality | | |
| Public Administration** | | |
| Health Care Management | | |
| Utilities*** | | |
| Communications | | |
| High Tech | | |
| Education | | |
| Manufacturing | | |

\* When most attendees will be dressed in this level of attire

\*\* Federal and local government

\*\*\* Electric, Gas, Telephone, Water

## TRADITIONAL BUSINESS ATTIRE

### Select the Traditional Businesss Attire when:

- Your organization's culture seems to be **formal**
- You desire to be perceived as **professional, most authoritative, credible, reliable/precise**
- You work in the following **industries** listed on this chart
- You have any of the listed **positions/jobs**
- You will be having any of the listed **interactions**

| Industry | Position/Job | Interactions |
|---|---|---|
| Banking | Upper mgt. | Clients: external |
| Insurance | Middle mgt. | Clients: internal |
| Legal/Accounting | Consultant | Meetings: external |
| Business Services | Sales-marketing | Presentations |
| Consulting Firms | | Representing company |
| Travel & Hospitality | | Negotiating a deal |
| Public Administration* | | Doing business overseas |
| Health Care Management | | Appearing in court |
| Utilities** | | |
| Communications | | |
| High Tech | | |

\* Federal and local government
\** Electric, Gas, Telephone, Water

## SPECIAL SITUATIONS

There are special situations, such as events, travel, entertainment, or job interviews, that require different types of clothing. Factors such as the weather, location, dress code expected for the event, and whether you will be a presenter, participant, etc., will determine the appropriate level of casual dress.

| Event | Weather | Dress Code Expected | Your Role | Appropriate Level |
|---|---|---|---|---|
| Conference | Any time of the year | Business casual | Participant | Smart |
| Industry Trade Show | Any time of year | Traditional business attire or business casual | Sales Representative | Traditional/Classic |
| | | | Exhibitor/Presenter | Classic/Smart |
| | | | Participant | Smart/Relaxed |
| Company picnic | Spring Summer | Casual | Guest/employee | Smart/Relaxed * |

*Be sure to review the list of inappropriate clothing for this level. An unprofessional appearance can damage the reputation that you have worked for all year.

## Travel

When traveling internationally, the Classic or Smart Levels will provide you with the comfort and professionalism required to represent your organization overseas. If your clients will pick you up at the airport, be sure that you take a jacket with you to meet them. First impressions count! Take into consideration the country weather and recommended business clothing. Do research before you travel; call the embassies of the countries to which you'll be traveling for information; search the Web; or read the many available books on international business etiquette.

For travel within the United States, follow a similar criteria. Take into account the weather and the type of clients you will visit. If you are going directly from the airport to your meeting, you may need to wear traditional business attire. If you can travel in more comfortable clothing, the Smart Level or the Classic Levels will be appropriate. Always take a jacket to ensure your professionalism during your trip. When you are traveling for business, you are representing your company, not only yourself.

During the week, most business travel requires the Classic Level. On weekends, the Smart Level is appropriate. If you travel on the weekends there is room for more flexibility. The Smart Level will be comfortable and appropriate if you will not meet your clients at the airport.

## Entertainment

When entertaining, the criteria for clothing selection includes:

Are you the host or hostess? Are you the guest? Client? Colleague? Supervisor? The host is the one who sets the tone for the appropriate dress. If you are inviting your client, let them know what the appropriate attire will be. If the event is at your office, explain what your company's dress policy is, business casual or traditional business attire. If the gathering is at a restaurant or golf club, give your client enough information about the place, the degree of formality, the type of cuisine, and the appropriate attire.

If you are a guest, ask questions about the appropriate attire and follow your host's advice. There is nothing worse than not being dressed appropriately when you are participating in a social event with business associates.

## Job Interview

When dressing for a job interview, ask the potential employer what is the appropriate attire for their organization. For most job interviews, you want to wear traditional business attire; or, if the organization is casual, the Classic Level, which includes a jacket, will be appropriate. When you arrive at the interview, if your potential employer is not wearing a jacket and you are the only one wearing one, take it off. This will make you look like a part of the team. Women need to pay special attention as to whether the potential employer allows women to wear pants. Ask, and when unsure, wear a skirted outfit.

# Details Count

Selecting the right casual clothing for the appropriate occasion is just half of the task of being well dressed for business. *Business Casual doesn't mean sloppy.* This is one of the most common mistakes professionals make. The way you care for your clothes, the condition of the pieces you wear, and your grooming are as essential as the choices you make. It is imperative to pay special attention to the overall look of your outfit. You want to give the message of neatness, cleanliness, and perfect grooming.

Remember that Business Casual is *business first* and *casual second*. When wearing business casual attire you must follow the basic guidelines of appropriate business dress. It means paying attention to the details such as proper fit, clothing care, grooming, and the use of accessories.

## Proper Fit

Proper fit is defined as the right size clothing for your body. Look for a *comfortable fit,* which is achieved when there is enough space between your body and your clothes so you can breathe and move easily.

A common problem that sabotages many people are clothes that are wrinkled, either too tight or too loose or baggy, which does not convey a professional/business look. It shows that the wearer did not pay attention to details, which could signal to clients, colleagues, and supervisors that the wearer will not pay attention to the details of their job.

Many men who usually have their traditional business clothes tailored to their perfect size, forget that with business casual clothing, tailoring becomes even more important. For example, casual pants need to be hemmed to your right length. Long-sleeved shirts have to fit at the right place on your wrist bone. Since most casual shirts come in only three sizes, you either need to have them altered to your right size, or look for a brand that makes the sleeves at the length that you require.

When selecting shirts, note that a fine collar is always stitched around the edges to stiffen and hold the folded material in place. The stitches should be in a single row and not more than one-quarter inch from the collar edge. The finer the shirt, the finer the stitching.

Women have a similar challenge. Some of the casual items are also available in three sizes—small, medium, and large. Often it is difficult to find one of these sizes that fits your body perfectly. Therefore, alterations for business casual clothing are as critical as they are for traditional business clothing. Skirts must fit comfortably on the hip area, without any visible horizontal lines; blouses and tops must have enough room and lie flat without pulling.

When selecting your collared shirts, blouses, and tops, pay attention to the length of your neck. Most casual shirts have standard collars which complement most face shapes. However, when selecting knit sweaters, remember that if your neck is short, the turtleneck will not look good on you. Instead, choose crew-neck or V-neck sweaters.

## Accessories

A rule of thumb when selecting accessories for your business casual attire is that *less is better*. Your shoes and hose or socks are the foundation of your outfit. Selecting the right style and color and keeping them in good condition is as important as attending to the other pieces of your outfit.

One tip for selecting hose and socks is to choose a color that blends with the two colors (either pant or skirt hemline and shoes) next to it. For example, with dark pants, wear dark socks and dark shoes; light socks would provide too much contrast thereby bringing attention to the feet. With a navy or black skirt, select dark shoes in navy or black and either gray or sheer hose; do not wear ivory or white for the same reason—you do not want too much contrast at the bottom.

### The Right Mix

Selecting the accessories for the right outfit is as important as choosing the right clothes. Even though you want versatility, remember that *all the pieces for an outfit have to belong to the same level of dressiness*. Avoid wearing outfits from the Classic Level with accessories from the Relaxed Level, and vice versa. For example, if wearing a jacket for the Classic Level, men and women need thin-soled shoes and neutral socks or hosiery. Women should not wear pantsuits with flats or sandals, and men should not wear sport jackets with penny loafers shoes. These combinations are as inappropriate as wearing jeans with a thin wing-tip shoe or high heels and hose.

The Smart Level is the level that gives you the most flexibility. Some pieces from this level can be worn with accessories from the Classic Level and some with the Relaxed Level. For example, you can wear khaki pants with shirts and medium-sole shoes or loafers. However, mixing clothing from the Smart Level with accessories from the Relaxed Level will make the total outfit relaxed. Example: Wearing khaki pants and a polo shirt with sandals makes the outfit relaxed.

When putting together the right combination between clothing and accessories, use these guidelines.

| Clothing | with | Comparable Accessories |
|---|---|---|
| Lightweight fabrics | | Thin, shiny, smooth material |
| Medium- to heavy-weight fabrics | | Medium to rough material |
| Matte-finish fabrics | | Matte-finish material |
| Shiny fabrics | | Shiny metal accessories |
| Items from one level | | Accessories from same level |

## The Essentials—Grooming

The canvas of the painting is the care of your body, hygiene, hair, skin care, makeup, etc. Good grooming becomes an essential way to facilitate good communication. For example, we certainly don't want to be distracted from our duties by an unruly lock of hair falling in our face, and we certainly don't want our customers to be distracted by this either. Good grooming—be it of hair, body, or face—keeps the focus where it belongs, on the business at hand.

The following pages provide illustrations with some of the most common dressing and grooming mistakes that can damage your professional image while wearing business casual clothing.

# WHAT IS WRONG WITH THESE PICTURES?

Unshaven, baggy pants,
shirt untucked

Tie and pants short, socks showing,
shirt pulling

# WHAT IS WRONG WITH THESE PICTURES?

T-shirt with inappropriate slogan
and tattoo

Jacket and pants too short,
socks showing

# WHAT IS WRONG WITH THESE PICTURES?

Tight jeans, messy hair,
cleavage showing

Short tight dress, strappy sandals,
too low neckline

# WHAT IS WRONG WITH THESE PICTURES?

Ripped jeans, tank top

Capri leggings, tube top, midriff
showing, strappy sandals

## How Do You Look?

We invite you to take a look at yourself in front of a long mirror, and let's see how your clothes fit and your clothing care and grooming measure up.

## Checklist for Men

### The Basics

- Clean shaven (no facial stubble)
- Hair should be short and clean; should not touch shirt collar
- Lint or dandruff are brushed off
- Hair in nose and ears are trimmed
- Well-trimmed mustache
- Beard recommended only to cover imperfections
- Fingernails are clean and short
- Heavy fragrances are avoided
- Clothes are clean and well pressed
- There are no buttons missing or falling hems
- Nothing is torn, stained, or discolored
- Tattoos are not visible

### Shirt

- No wrinkles in collar, cuffs, or facing
- If buttoned, collar loose enough for one finger to fit in neckline
- Collar of shirt stands ¼" to ½" above collar of jacket
- Sleeve extends ⅛" to ¼" below the jacket
- Short sleeves end at elbow
- No sleeveless shirts or tank tops
- No T-shirts with inappropriate messages

### Pants

- Bottom of pants are just breaking in the front
- Bottom of pants cover top of shoes in back
- If pleated, pleats lie flat and are not open

- If uncuffed, tapered toward the back
- Fall straight from buttocks
- Top of pants fit on the waist
- Pockets remain flat, no bulging
- Pants well pressed
- No holes

### Tie

- Ends at the belt line
- Width same size or smaller than jacket lapel
- Pattern size not larger than the size of four quarters
- No tie tack or clip
- Tie knot is balanced with shirt collar
- Four-in-hand knot for thicker tie fabrics with all collars

### Jacket

- Does not wrinkle across the back
- Length covers buttocks
- Collar lies flat against the shirt
- Sleeve length at wrist bone
- Top-stitching is even, no loose threads
- Leather or metal buttons on sport coat

### Sweater/Vest

- Crew or V-neck sweaters, loose not baggy
- Turtleneck for average to long neck
- Vest always worn with shirt

### Shoes

- Highly polished if shiny leather for Classic Level
- Oxfords and suede leather must be clean
- Dark color: black, cordovan, or brown
- Thin, medium, or thick soles to coordinate with outfit—Smart and Relaxed Levels

- Tie or slip-on tassel loafers for sport coat
- Penny loafers or loafers with low vamp for outfits without a jacket
- Always in good condition

## Socks

- Always wear socks
- Color blends with trousers and shoes
- Subtle patterns for Classic Level
- Argyles or other patterns for Smart and Relaxed Levels only
- Long enough to cover calf, no skin showing

## Jewelry

- No bracelets, chains, or fancy rings
- No earrings
- Simple and elegant are best choices
- Gold or silver face watch with leather or metal band
  (for Classic and Smart Levels)
- Sport watch for Relaxed Level only

## Other Accessories

- Pocket square that complements tie, never identical to it
- No tinted glasses
- Braces in neutral color or pattern, to complement tie
- No clip-on suspenders
- Never wear braces with belt
- Belt color blends with shoes
  - No large buckles
  - Simple, classic design
  - Must be in good condition and not worn out
  - Fastened on third or middle hole

**Tip:** Invest in a full-length mirror and inspect the total picture and the details.

## Checklist for Women

### The Basics

- Simple, carefree hair styles
- No roots showing with colored hair
- No extreme fashion hair styles and colors
- Pulled back hair if it falls below the shoulders
- No lint or dandruff
- Makeup color selection application is subtle and blended
- Fingernails are clean and short to medium-length
- No overly bright colors (fuchsia-orange-purple) in nail polish
- No chipped nail polish
- No dark lingerie with light clothing
- No buttons missing or a falling hem
- No heavy fragrances

### Jacket

- No wrinkles across the back or under the collar
- Buttons easily
- Long sleeves at wrist bone
- Short sleeve at elbow
- Does not pull across the back

### Blouse/Tops

- Long sleeve should be at wrist bone
- Short sleeve at elbow or half-arm length
- Buttons must remain closed with at least 1" of fabric on each side of the bust line
- Longer than the hip bone—no skin showing at waist
- No revealing necklines front or back
- Neckline (2" above cleavage)
- No tight tops and sweaters
- Cardigan style should be able to button or zip comfortably
- No see-through or bare midriff

### Pants

- Pleats remain closed
- Zippers and closings must lie flat
- Long enough to break in front
- Do not wrinkle across the front
- Fall straight from buttocks
- Waistband loose enough to allow two fingers to be inserted
- Panty line must not show

### Dress

- Conservative neckline (2" above cleavage)
- Medium to small print

### Skirt

- Pleats do not pull open
- No crease or pull across break of leg
- Should easily turn around your body
- Straight skirts should hang from buttocks in a straight line and not curve under
- Not shorter than "around the knee"
- Loose enough for two fingers to be inserted in waistband
- No high slit in skirt
- No slip showing below hemline or between slit

### Shoes

- Select neutral or color shades that coordinate with hemline
- Avoid too high or narrow heels
- Keep heels in good condition
- Keep shiny leather shoes polished

### Hose

- Always wear hose or socks for a more professional look
- Hose color does not bring attention to leg area
- Neutral color hose that blends with hemline

- Hose color in nude, same shade as shoes or lighter, never darker
- No colored hose (red, purple, pink)
- No patterned or textured hose
- No hose runs, snags, or bagginess

### Jewelry

- Choose small to medium earrings, simple styles
- Avoid earrings larger than the size of a quarter
- Avoid dangling or large hooped earrings
- Avoid noisy jewelry or pieces that move
- Avoid too many pieces
- Avoid tinted glasses

**Tip:** Invest in a full-length mirror and inspect the total picture and the details.

## Clothing Care

Here are a few tips to ensure that your clothing looks its best and lasts a long time.

### Tailored Clothing

- Hang clothing on heavy plastic or wood hangers. *Do not hang clothes on wire hangers.*
- Allow wool clothing to "breathe" on a hanger (not in a closet) for 24 hours after wearing. This will help evaporate moisture and restore the shape of the garment. If you smoke, they may need to air for 48 hours. If the wrinkles do not come out of the clothes, ask your dry cleaner to "press only." Pressing is less damaging to wool fibers compared to cleaning solutions.

- Avoid dry-cleaning your wool clothing unless it is soiled. If your clothing is soiled, take it to the cleaners immediately and let them know what the stain consists of.
- Always dry-clean a matching jacket and pants together.

**Cotton and machine-washable clothing**

*Prior to washing:*

- Examine and repair any loose buttons, seams, or tears so that the washing machine doesn't do any further damage.
- Empty pockets of everything and close buttons, snaps, and zippers.
- Pre-treat any stains.
- Use delicate cycle for tops, blouses, shirts, and regular cycle for heavy cotton trousers or denim.

*Washing:*

- Read the care label for specific instructions such as water temperature.
- Sort clothing into whites and colors (all others).
- Don't overload machine. It is better to do two smaller loads than one large load. Clothing will get cleaner and there will be less wear and tear on the garments.

*Drying:*

- Allow cotton and microfiber garments to dry until the wrinkles are gone (about 75 percent dry). Remove clothes immediately and hang to dry until they are cool. Hang up/or fold immediately, button top button, smooth out any wrinkles or press lightly.
- Avoid overloading the dryer. This will cause wrinkling. A few smaller loads will dry faster than one large one.
- Dry synthetics (man-made fabrics such as fleece) separate from cottons. This will prevent the lint from the natural fibers from getting on the synthetic fabrics.
- Make sure to clean your lint filter often. A clogged filter will result in clothes needing longer drying time.

*Pressing:*

- Everything you wear will look better if it is pressed. If you are good with the iron and enjoy it, then press your own clothing. If not, spend the money at your dry cleaners. Remember, just because you are dressing casual, does not mean you should compromise on neatness.

### Hosiery / Socks

**Women:** Panty hose should either be washed by hand using a mild detergent or in the washing machine on a gentle cycle. If you choose the latter, the hose should always be put in a mesh bag to prevent runs. Hose should then be hung up to air dry.

**Men:** Wool socks can be machine washed, but should be line dried to prolong their life. Cotton socks can be machine washed and dried in the dryer.

### Shoe Care

- Having clean, well-polished shoes is just as important as having clean, pressed clothing.
- It is best to have at least two pairs of work shoes that you can wear every other day. By alternating shoes, you allow the leather to breathe and dry out. By following the tips below, your shoes can last for several years.
- Keep all of your shoes on wooden shoe trees. The shoe trees serve two functions: they absorb perspiration and maintain the shape of the shoes. You can double the life of your leather shoes by using a wooden shoe tree.
- Polish shoes either yourself or by a professional whenever needed.
- Replace heels, soles, and toe tips when necessary.

# 9

# Wardrobe for Women

Building your Business Casual Wardrobe can be an easy task by following these three steps.

**Step One: Inventory**

The first step in building a wardrobe is to take inventory. The same way you look in your refrigerator and cabinets before heading to the supermarket, you need to review what you have first before you can decide what you need to buy.

Approach your closet and drawers *as if they belong to somebody else.* Bring three large bags. One for items to be tossed, one for repairs, and one to be donated to somebody else. Carefully examine every item. Try things on if you haven't worn them in a while. Look for stains, tears, missing buttons. Give careful consideration to the following items:

• Gifts that you've never worn
• Items that were purchased on sale but do not reflect your style
• Items in colors that are not flattering
• Anything you haven't worn in the last year to year and a half
• Items that you're hoping to fit into "sometime soon."

These items of clothing can be donated to a woman who would be very happy to have them. Look in Chapter 11 for the names and phone numbers of organizations that provide clothing to women in need. A few organizations are specifically geared toward helping women prepare for job interviews and work. You can also check your local yellow pages.

If you have a large amount of clothing, you may need to do this exercise over several days. It is best to review the clothing from the current season and save the other seasons for another day. Do not stop until you have reviewed everything in your closets/drawers and made decisions about what to do with the clothing.

**Step Two: What You Need**

The second step is to compare what you have with what you need. Begin by looking at the wardrobe charts in this chapter. Depending on which level you wear most often, you will be able to see what you need. Notice if you have the basics or too many bottoms and not enough tops. Next, start to look at how many outfits you can make with the pieces you have from your business and casual wardrobes. Look at Chapter 5 for combinations and illustrations. Your goal is to form capsule wardrobes. These are groupings of items that can be mixed and matched to create several outfits.

A capsule wardrobe consists of garments of the same fabric weight, texture, and overall quality. A capsule has four to five colors. Two neutrals and two brights. The items need to blend in color, fabric, and style. Each item should work with three other pieces.

The core of a capsule wardrobe consists of the following mix and match items:

- One solid three-piece suit (jacket, skirt, and pants) in a neutral color made in all-weather wool/microfiber
- A pair of khaki or cotton twill pants
- A pair of jeans—if your office permits them
- Twin-sweater set in cotton or silk knit

- A solid white blouse with long sleeves that buttons in the front
- A striped silk/cotton knit top
- A striped blouse with long sleeves that buttons in front
- A colored turtleneck or mock turtleneck
- Two to three solid tops (see individual wardrobe charts)
- Accessories to pull the outfit together: shoes, handbag, earrings, necklace, pin, or scarf
- Scarves are especially useful in creating a coordinated outfit, i.e., blue sweater with khaki pants and a mixed blue, khaki, red, and white printed scarf.

The key to making your capsules work is that all of the fabrics need to be the same weight, texture, and overall quality, (i.e. silk knit/wool). Be careful about pairing cotton and wool and linen/wool together; it may not look right. Also, the patterns and size of the designs need to work in harmony with the solid neutrals.

**Step Three: Key Bridge Pieces**

The third step is to look for key bridge pieces. These are items that can be worn with your traditional business attire and your casual attire. For example, look at your matching suits. How many different outfits can you make using the jacket from your traditional or casual business suit? How about the pants? Match your suit pants with a sweater set and there is another outfit. Take your solid or patterned jacket and put it together with more casual pants. Look at Chapter 5's illustrations and review the combination list.

**Key Bridge Items Include:**

- Single-breasted all-weather wool jackets/blazers
- Wool/wool-blend pants
- Wool/wool-blend skirts
- Sweater sets
- Solid silk/rayon/ blouses
- Printed silk/rayon blouses

# CAPSULE WARDROBE

**Items, clockwise**
Solid suit jacket
Solid skirt
Solid suit pants
Khaki pants
Twin-sweater shell and
cardigan

# CAPSULE WARDROBE

White, long-sleeved blouse

Striped, long-sleeved blouse

Horizontal, striped
cotton knit top

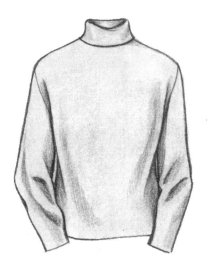

Colored turtleneck

## ACCESSORIES

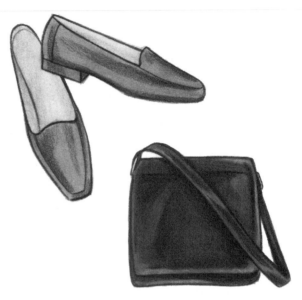

**Clockwise from top**
Medium-heel pumps
Trouser shoes
Handbag
Belt
Casual necklace, earrings, pin
Scarves

# MIXED AND MATCHED ITEMS: COMPLETE OUTFITS

## MIXED AND MATCHED ITEMS: COMPLETE OUTFITS

## MIXED AND MATCHED ITEMS: COMPLETE OUTFITS

*If permitted by your organization

# Key Elements of a Woman's CLASSIC LEVEL Wardrobe

## Pantsuits /Pants

Pantsuits/pants in all-weather wool or microfibers
Pantsuits in neutral colors or subtle patterns (2-4)*
Wool pants in solids or pattern (5-7)

## Blazers

Plain with no detailing or metal buttons (2)
Navy blue plus one or more of the following colors: black, brown, beige, taupe, gray, or
    subtle pattern in neutral color (fabric should be 100 percent wool, silk, or microfiber).

## Skirts (2-4)

Straight, flowing, wrap, or A-line skirt in pattern or solid

## Tops (8-10)

Silk crew neck
Cotton button-down blouse
Sweater sets in cotton, silk, or wool knit
Turtleneck sweater in cotton, silk, or wool knit

## Shoes (thin heels /soles) (3-5+)

Smooth leather trouser shoes, loafers
Any updated style with low or stacked heel

## Handbag and Tote (2+)

Structured leather or microfiber bag and tote in color and texture that matches with shoes

## Accessories

Updated leather belts that coordinate in style and color with shoes and handbag
Necklaces in gold or silver (the best quality you can afford), pearls, or semi-precious stones
Earrings in pearl or metal that flatters your skin tone
Scarves (if you feel comfortable with them) in colors that coordinate with your suits, tops,
    and pants
One watch in gold or silver metal

*Numbers in ( ) are the recommended number of items.

# Key Elements of a Woman's SMART LEVEL Wardrobe

## Pants / Shorts

Wool, wool-blend, microfiber pants in neutral solid colors or subtle patterns (2-4)
Khakis, twill, corduroy pants (3-5)
Walking shorts with jacket (1-2)

## Skirts / Dresses (3-5)

Straight, flowing, wrap, or A-line skirt in pattern or solid
Dresses—solid, florals, geometric
Jumper in cotton, knit, wool

## Tops / Vests / Sweaters (8-10)

Silk crew neck
Cotton button-down blouse
Sweater sets in cotton, silk, or wool knit
Turtleneck sweater in cotton, silk, or wool knit
Pullover crew or V-neck sweater
Cardigan sweater

## Shoes (3-5+)

Thin to medium heels/soles
Leather, suede, microfiber trouser shoes, loafers, moccasins
Any updated style with flat, low, stacked, or platform heel

## Handbag and Tote (2+)

Unstructured leather, suede, Coach™ type or microfiber bag and tote in color and texture
that matches with shoes

## Accessories

Updated leather or suede belts that coordinate in style and color with shoes and handbag
Necklaces—medium size in matte-finish gold or silver, craft-type design, ceramic, beads,
ethnic motifs
Earrings in gold, silver, pearl, or matte-finish stone in hoop, short dangling, or drop style
Scarves (if you feel comfortable with them) in colors that coordinate with your tops and
pants
Watch with silver or metal face/band or metal face with leather band

## Key Elements of a Woman's RELAXED LEVEL Wardrobe

### Pants /Shorts

Jeans in blue, black, and white (2-4)
Khakis, twill, chinos, denim,  (3-5)
Walking shorts to the knee (1-3)

### Skirts /Jumper /Dresses

Denim skirt or twill jumper (2-4)
Short sleeve/sleeveless dress in solid, floral, geometric print (2-4)

### Tops /Vests /Sweaters (8-10)

Cotton blouse or T-shirt
T-shirt without messages
Denim blouse
Sweater sets in cotton, silk, or wool knit
Turtleneck sweater in cotton, silk, or wool knit
Pullover crew or V-neck sweater
Vest—knit or fabric

### Shoes (3-5+)

Thin, medium, or thick heels/soles
Leather, suede, woven, microfiber trouser shoes, loafers, moccasins
Any updated style with flat, low, stacked, or platform heel

### Handbag and Tote (2+)

Unstructured leather, suede, Coach™ type, knit, canvas, or microfiber bag and tote in
    color and texture that matches with shoes

### Accessories

Belts—updated leather, suede, or any that coordinate in style and color with shoes and
    handbag
Necklaces—medium size in matte-finish gold or silver, craft-type design, ceramic, beads,
    ethnic motifs
Earrings in gold, silver, pearl, or matte-finish stone in hoop, short dangling, or drop style.
Scarves (if you feel comfortable with them) in silk, colors that
    coordinate with your tops and pants
Watch with silver or metal face and leather band or sports/fashion watch, i.e., Swatch

## Shopping Tips

When putting together a wardrobe of business casual attire, it is best to keep many of the same shopping strategies that you would use in buying traditional clothing.

Buying clothing should be seen as an investment. If you make good decisions, your clothing will last for several years. Poor choices translate into expensive mistakes. The best investment pieces are items that are in classic styles with simple lines and no detailing. They will last the longest and can be updated to look current with accessories.

---

### Recommendations for all purchases

*Excellent Quality:* Always choose quality over quantity. You will win in the long run.

*Classic Design:* Your clothing will never look dated.

*Versatility:* Make sure each item can be worn with at least three other items.

*Colors:* Start with a base of neutrals (black, beige, taupe, gray, navy) before moving into brights, lights, and pastels.

*Body Type:* Make sure the clothing is flattering to your body. Specifically, make sure that the clothing highlights your "assets" and hides your "liabilities."

*Proper Fit:* Make sure the clothing fits well. If it needs alterations, have them done immediately.

*Accessories:* Use accessories to update your look, create your own personal style, and pull your outfit together. Make sure when wearing Classic Level that you keep all of the accessories at the same level of dressiness. For Smart and Relaxed Levels, you have more freedom in combining levels of dressiness.

---

Learn how to determine quality by looking for:

- Matching seams, especially with prints and patterns
- How the buttonholes were finished on the inside of cardigan sweaters and twin sets
- Lining that is tacked to the outer fabric in shoulders, armholes, and sleeve hems
- Buttonholes neatly finished without loose threads
- Zippers that will not unzip even if the tab is down
- Hemlines that hang evenly
- Quality buttons: bone, leather, covered, or mother of pearl
- Clean, finished seams that do not pull or wrinkle
- Pockets that lie flat

### Other tips while shopping

- If you find something that you love and it's perfect, buy two or buy the second one in another color.
- Shop with a plan. Know what you need and start there before heading to what you want.
- If you want to update your wardrobe with something new and trendy, don't spend a lot of money; go to the high-end stores to look around for ideas and buy the lower priced version.
- Find the best dressed/put together salesperson to help you—preferably someone with the same size/coloring as you.
- Only buy things that are perfect "10s". The right color, shape, and style for you.
- Choose only those items that fit in with your capsule wardrobe. New purchases can be a lighter or darker shade of your original neutral or bright colors, as long as they can blend with what you have.

**Stay on purpose!**
Don't get sidetracked and not buy what you set out for.

## Comfort

- Buy shoes in the middle of the day when your feet have expanded.
- Carry bottled water with you to avoid dehydration.
- Eat before you begin shopping and stop to eat if you're spending more than two hours.

## WOMEN'S WARDROBE SUMMARY

When building your Business Casual Wardrobe think:

- Excellent quality
- Classic designs
- Neutral colors for main pieces
- Bright, light, and prints for other pieces
- Versatility: purchase only pieces that will mix with at least 3 others
- Accessories for individuality and updating

When expanding your corporate wardrobe, use your existing pieces and mix them with items from your business casual wardrobe:

**Mix your basic solid neutral suit jacket with a:**

Knit top
Blouse and vest
Scarf or necklace
Solid or patterned pants

**Mix any neutral color skirt with a:**

Printed blouse
Knit top and jacket
Sweater set
Blouse/vest and/or jacket
Scarf or interesting belt

**Mix any neutral color skirted suit with a:**

Cotton solid blouse
Sweater or knit top
Colorful or printed top

**Mix any neutral color or patterned pants with a:**

Cotton blouse
Sweater or knit top
Blouse and vest
Solid or patterned blazer
Sweater set

# Wardrobe for Men

Building your Business Casual Wardrobe can be an easy task by following these three steps.

**Step One: Inventory**

The first step in building a wardrobe is to take inventory. The same way you look in your toolbox before heading to the hardware store, you need to review what you have first before you can decide what you need to buy.

Look at your closet and drawers *as if they belong to somebody else.* Bring three large bags. One for items to be thrown away, one for repairs, and one to be donated to somebody else. Carefully examine every item. Try things on if you haven't worn them in a while. Look for stains, tears, missing buttons. Give careful consideration to the following items:

• Gifts you've never worn
• Anything you haven't worn in the last one or two years
• Items that you're hoping to fit into "sometime soon."

If you have a large amount of clothing, you may need to do this exercise over several days. It is best to review the clothing from the current season and save the other seasons for another day. Do not stop until you have reviewed everything in your closets/drawers and made decisions about what to do with the clothing. If you decide to donate your clothing, look in the yellow pages for organizations that provide clothing to men in need.

## Step Two: What You Need

The second step is to compare your current business wardrobe to the wardrobe charts in this chapter. Depending on which level you wear most often, you will be able to see what you need. Look at your blazers and trousers. Do you have lots of pants and just one blazer? Do you have a closet filled with khakis and almost no wool pants, twills, corduroys? If you wear Classic Level, you probably need to buy a couple more blazers and nice pants. If you wear Smart or Relaxed Levels most often, you might need to buy more casual shirts. Remember, some of your traditional dress shirts in white or stripes will be too dressy for business casual.

Next, start to look at the number of outfits you can make with the pieces you have from your business and casual wardrobes. Look at Chapter 6 for combinations and illustrations. Your goal is to form capsule wardrobes. These are groupings of items that can be mixed and matched to create several outfits.

A capsule wardrobe consists of clothing of the same fabric, weight and overall quality. A capsule has four to five colors. Two neutrals and two or three bright and light colors. The items need to blend in color, fabric, and style. Each item in the capsule should work with three other pieces.

The core of a capsule wardrobe consists of the following mix and match items:

- One navy blue single-breasted blazer
- One sport coat in either tweed, plaid, herringbone, or check
- Two pairs of solid wool or wool-blend pants
- Two pairs of khaki pants
- A pair of jeans, if your office permits them

- Two dress shirts in solid or print
- Two polo shirts in solid or print
- Three ties in creative patterns
- Two sweaters in crew, turtleneck, or V-neck
- Two leather belts in black, brown, or cordovan
- Two pairs of leather shoes in black, cordovan, or brown. Soles can be leather or rubber in thin to medium thickness.

### Step Three: Key Bridge Pieces

The third step is to look for key bridge pieces. These are items that can be worn with your traditional business attire and your casual attire. For example, your navy blue blazer can be dressed down by wearing it with a solid blue shirt, turtleneck, shirt and vest, shirt and crew neck sweater, polo sweater. Look at Chapter 6's illustrations and review the combination lists.

### Key bridge items include:

- Jackets: Single-breasted wool, cashmere, linen/silk blend
- Sport coats/jackets/blazers
- Pants: all-weather wool, wool blends, silk blends
- Dress shirts: solid shirts in medium to dark colors, stripes
- Sport shirts, polo shirts, banded-collar shirts

## CAPSULE WARDROBE

Above: Blazer
Sport coat
Below: Dark wool pants
Medium color wool pants

# CAPSULE WARDROBE

Above: Dark khakis
Medium color khakis
Jeans*
Below: Dark long-sleeved shirt
Striped shirt

*If permitted by
your organization

## CAPSULE WARDROBE

Above: Printed polo shirt
Solid polo shirt
Below: Crew neck sweater
V-neck sweater

## CAPSULE WARDROBE

Above: Creative
patterned ties
Middle: Smooth leather belt
Embossed belt
Below: Slip-on tassel
penny loafers

## MIXED AND MATCHED ITEMS: COMPLETE OUTFITS

# MIXED AND MATCHED ITEMS: COMPLETE OUTFITS

# MIXED AND MATCHED ITEMS: COMPLETE OUTFITS

If permitted by your organization

# Key Elements of a Man's CLASSIC LEVEL Wardrobe

**Blazers/sports coats** (2-3)*

Tailored single breasted in solid or pattern
100% wool, wool blend, cashmere, silk/linen blend

**Pants** (5-8)

Pants in all-weather wool/wool blend in neutral solid colors or subtle patterns, i.e., navy, black, gray

**Shirts/Vests/Sweaters** (8-10)

Cotton, cotton-blend dress shirts in solid, striped, or patterned
Sweater vest in solid color
Pullover crew or V-neck sweater
Turtleneck or mock turtleneck

**Ties** (5-10)

Stripes, fine to bold
Abstracts
Conversational patterned ties

**Shoes** (3-5+)

Thin heels/soles
Oxfords (lace up or wing tip)
Loafers with tassels or buckles
Leather monk strap

**Accessories**

Smooth or embossed leather belts in same color as shoes
Watch with gold or silver face and metal or leather band

*Numbers in ( ) are the recommended number of items.

# Key Elements of a Man's SMART LEVEL Wardrobe

**Pants** (5-8)

All-weather wool/wool blend in neutral solids or pattern
Flannel
Khaki
Twill
Chinos
Microfiber

**Shirts with Collars** (8-10)

Cotton or cotton-blend dress and sport shirts in solid, striped, or patterned
Polo shirts in different colors and patterns
Banded collar

**Vests** (1-2)

Knit or silk/wool blend: solid or patterned

**Sweaters** (3-6)

Pullover crew or V-neck sweater in wool, cashmere, or fine cotton
Cardigan
Turtlenecks

**Shoes** (3-5+)

Thin to medium leather or rubber heels/soles
Oxfords (lace up or wing tip)
Tasseled or penny loafer
Leather monk strap
Suede leather oxfords

**Accessories**

Smooth or embossed leather belts in same color as shoes
Watch with gold or silver face and metal or leather band

## Key Elements of a Man's RELAXED LEVEL Wardrobe

**Pants** (5-8)

Jeans
Khaki
Twill
Corduroy

**Shirts with or without collars** (8-10)

Cotton / cotton blend, linen, or denim shirts in stripes, plaids
T-shirts with or without pockets
Polo shirts
Banded collar

**Vests** (1-2)

Vests in wool knit, cashmere, cotton, denim

**Sweaters/Turtlenecks** (3-5)

Cardigan sweater
Pullover crew or V-neck sweater in wool, cashmere, or fine cotton
Turtlenecks/mock turtleneck

**Shoes** (3)

Medium to thick leather or rubber heels/soles
Penny loafers
Suede or leather lace up or monk straps
Sneakers

**Accessories**

Belts (2-3): woven, canvas, canvas with leather trim
Watch with gold or silver face and metal or leather band, sports watch,
    nautical styles, or Swatch (plastic band)

## Shopping Tips

When putting together a wardrobe of business casual attire, it is best to keep many of the same shopping strategies that you would use in buying traditional clothing.

Buying clothing should be seen as an investment. If you make good decisions, your clothing will last for several years. Poor choices translate into expensive mistakes.

---

**Recommendations for all purchases**

*Excellent Quality:*   Always choose quality over quantity. You will win in the long run.

*Proper Fit:*   If you are in between sizes in blazers, i.e., almost a long, but not quite, buy the larger size and have alterations made.

- Have all of your alterations made in the store where you are buying the clothes.

- Try to find a brand that fits your body, particularly your sleeve length if the shirt is only available in small, medium, and large.

*Versatility:*   Make sure each item can be worn with at least three other items.

---

## Recommendations for all purchases (cont.)

*Colors:*      Purchase pants and jackets in neutrals (navy, gray, beige, taupe, camel). Add colors and prints for shirts, ties, and sweaters.

*Accessories:*    Use accessories to update your look, create your own personal style, and pull your outfit together.

Make sure that when you are wearing the Classic Level that you keep all of the accessories at the same level of dressiness. For example, wear a smooth calfskin leather belt with smooth leather lace-up shoes.

For the Smart Levels you have more freedom in combining levels of dressiness with the texture of your shoes and belts. Just be careful not to combine a very casual woven or rope belt with wool trousers. Those belts will work well only with khaki or cotton pants.

For the Relaxed Level, you also have freedom in combining accessories and pieces of clothing. You can mix pieces from the Smart and the Relaxed Levels. Avoid wearing very dressy accessories such as wing-tip shoes with your jeans.

## MEN'S WARDROBE SUMMARY

When building your Business Casual Wardrobe think:
- Excellent quality
- Solid colors for pants and jackets
- Patterns for jackets/sweaters
- Medium to dark colors and prints, stripes, checks for shirts
- Versatility: purchase only pieces that match with at least 3 others

When expanding your corporate wardrobe, use your existing pieces
and mix them with items from your business casual wardrobe:

**Mix your basic navy or camel blazer with a:**

Colored dress or sport shirt
Patterned shirt
Sweater
Vest (with a shirt)

**Mix your basic khaki pants with a:**

Polo shirt
Sweater and knit shirt
Shirt and vest
Colored shirt
Banded-collar shirt

**Mix your tweed or plaid sport coat with a:**

Colored dress or sport shirt
Colorful tie
Turtleneck sweater
Polo shirt

**Mix your wool pants (*not* from your suits) with a:**

Dress or sport buttoned-down shirt
Plaid shirt
Turtleneck
Shirt and vest
Sweater and knit shirt

# Resources

The clothing industry has responded to the trend of business casual with an increase in casual attire available to the consumer through the following: retail stores, specialty stores, catalogs, direct sales by consultants, and shopping on the Internet.

Below is a list of resources that will help you in building your business casual wardrobe. If you prefer to visit stores, look for one that carries the styles and the prices that most fit your budget. Many stores offer catalogs that are either published regularly or every season to encourage phone orders. Most stores also have their own Web page and customer service representatives with information to facilitate your shopping.

## Stores for Men and Women

Barneys: 888-222-7639
Banana Republic: www.bananarepublic.com, 888-277-8953
Bloomingdale's: www.bloomingdales.com, 800-777-0000
Brooks Brothers: www.brooksbrothers.com, 800-274-1815
Eddie Bauer: www.eddiebauer.com, 800-426-6253
Gap: www.gap.com
JCPenney: www.jcpenney.com, 800-222-6161
J. Crew: www.jcrew.com, 800-562-0258
Liz Claiborne: www.lizclaiborne.com, 800-578-7070
Loehmann's: Look for store in your area
Macy's: www.macys.com, 800-431-9644
Neiman Marcus: 800-944-9888
Nordstrom: www.nordstrom.com, 800-285-5800
Lord & Taylor: Look for store in your area
Old Navy Co.: 800-Old-Navy
Ralph Lauren: Look for store in your area
Saks Fifth Avenue: 800-345-3454
Sears: www.sears.com, 800-549-4505
Stein Mart: www.steinmart.com
Target: 612-304-8637
The Limited: Look for store in your area

## Stores for Women

Ann Taylor: Look for store in your area
Talbots: www.talbots.com, 800-882-5268
Petite Sophisticated: 203-741-0771
Tall Classics: www.tallclassics.com, 800-345-1958

## Stores for Men

**Joseph A. Bank:** www.josbank.com, 800-285-2265
**Today's Man:** www.todaysman.com, 703-385-5670

## Catalogs for Women

**Barrie Pace Ltd.:** www.barriepace.com, 800-441-6011
**C.W. Clifford & Wills:** 800-922-0114
**JCPenney:** www.jcpenney.com, 800-222-6161
**J. Crew:** www.jcrew.com, 800-562-0258
**Land's End, First Person Singular:** www.landsend.com, 800-966-4434
**L.L. Bean:** www.llbean.com, 800-341-4341
**Norm Thompson:** www.normthompson.com, 800-547-1160
**Sears:** www.sears.com, 800-549-4505
**Spiegel:** www.spiegel.com, 800-345-4500

## Catalogs for Men

**Brooks Brothers:** www.brooksbrothers.com, 800-274-1815
**Eddie Bauer:** www.eddiebauer.com, 800-426-8020
**JCPenney:** www.jcpenney.com, 800-222-6161
**J. Crew:** www.jcrew.com, 800-562-0258
**Johnston & Murphy:** www.johnstonandmurphy.com, 800-424-2854
**Joseph A. Bank:** www.josbank.com, 800-285-2265
**L.L. Bean:** www.llbean.com, 800-341-4341
**Paul Fredrick:** www.paulfredrick.com, 800-247-1417
**Sears:** www.sears.com, 800-549-4505

## Nonprofit Organizations to Donate Business Clothing

Attitudes & Attire
Dallas, TX: 214-630-1667

Bottomless Closet®
Chicago, IL: 312-527-9664
New York, NY: 212-563-2499

Career Closet
San Jose, CA: 408-448-3215

Clothes The Deal
Los Angeles, CA: 213-688-1020

Corporate Collection
Pittsburgh, PA: 412-967-0399

Dress for Success
www.dressforsuccess.org

Images for Success
San Rafael, CA: 415-457-2114

Positive Impressions, Inc.
Boston, MA: 617-266-2356

Success, Inc.
Cincinnati, OH: 513-961-7593

Suitability
Lowell, MA: 978-934-8898

Suited for Change
Washington, DC: 202-293-0351

Suited For Success
New York, NY: 212-682-3774

Working Wardrobe
Philadelphia, PA: 215-568-6693

## Direct Sales: Sold one-on-one

**Carlisle:** 212-246-4275
**Doncaster:** www.doncaster.com, 800-669-3662
**French Raggs:** 800-347-5270

## Seminars for Corporations, Organizations, Universities, and Colleges

For information on Business Casual seminars, presentations, and consulting based on this book contact:

**Business Casual Publications, L.C.:**
www.businesscasualdress.com

*Washington Office:* 703-560-3950

*New York Office:* 914-478-3827

## Other Materials for Image Consultants and Trainers

For materials for your presentations and seminars on Business Casual contact:

**Business Casual Publications, L.C.:**
www.businesscasualdress.com

*Washington Office:* 703-560-3950

*New York Office:* 914-478-3827

# 12

# Developing and Managing a Business Casual Policy

Most organizations decide to implement a casual dress policy as a no-cost employee benefit to create an environment that is comfortable for employees and conducive to open communication. At the same time, organizations need to ensure that this new benefit becomes a morale booster and not a costly company image breaker.

We have defined a five-step process to assist you and your organization in implementing a successful Business Casual Policy.

1. Policy Definition
2. Information/Communication
3. Education
4. Application
5. Follow-Up/Enforcement

In order for a policy to be effective, all five steps need to be included. If you already have a policy or have started a program and are having challenges, review the following steps. You will determine which might have been left out, and will find ideas on how to address specific challenges.

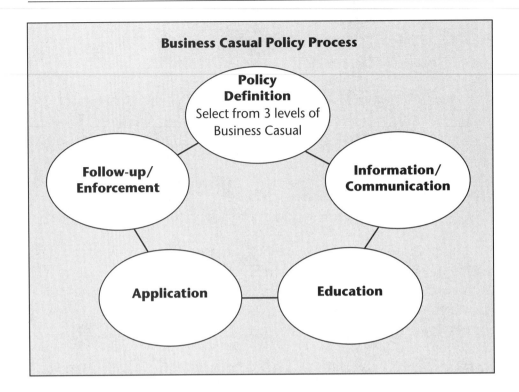

## 1. POLICY DEFINITION

Background: Many organizations have allowed employees to wear business casual clothing either on Fridays, on certain days or weeks during the year, during the summer months, or on special holidays. Other organizations have permitted business casual attire for specific departments or locations on a trial basis. After evaluating the results, most organizations decide to extend the policy during longer periods of the year or to make it standard for the whole organization year round.

The most common reasons for extending the policy are:

■ Employees enjoyed the freedom and comfort of dressing casually when they were allowed to do so.

- It may have improved employee morale.

- Employees asked for it.

- The organization wants to follow the industry trend of allowing employees to dress more casually.

Whatever the situation, it is important to clarify the specific reasons for your organization because this will be valuable information when defining and writing the policy. It is helpful to explain to your employees the reasons for introducing a business casual policy.

When defining a dress code for business casual, your organization has to establish the general parameters. Depending on your organization's culture, the general guidelines will include the answers to these questions:

- Will business casual be optional, or do you expect all employees to dress casually at all times?

- Will it apply to all employees of the organization or only in certain departments?

- What will be accepted as business casual for your company?

- Which one of the three levels will be appropriate for your business? Most organizations accept two of the Business Casual Levels defined in this book: Classic Level, which includes jackets, and Smart Level, which includes layers.

- Will your organization include the Relaxed Level which allows jeans, T-shirts, and sneakers? This is a critical definition as many organizations draw the line on these items.

Defining the general parameters is usually easier when you think of what you don't want to see your employees wearing. Make a sketchy list of these items for further discussion.

Depending on your organization's culture, the general parameters may be decided by upper management or by a *task force* that is created for this purpose. If your organization decides to create a task force made up of diverse employees, be sure to invite employees of different departments, including those areas with high- and low-customer contact. A task force will facilitate the process so the employees will own the policy and consequently will adhere to it.

Either the upper management team or the task force will work on the policy definition based on the general parameters.

Depending on your organization, you can choose between a general policy or a specific policy.

## A. Defining General Policy

Many times, a brief set of parameters will be sufficient. The policy may include only general guidelines in which case you want to produce a one- or two-page *draft document* that covers the following elements:

### 1. Purpose

- The reasons why your organization is implementing this new way of dressing for work.

- Considerations about your organization goals and image. If employees have asked for this new way of dress for work, include wording such as *"We've listened to your comments and suggestions…"*

### 2. Timing

- Days of the week, daily, Fridays, all year round, etc.

## 3. Definition

■ Description of what will be considered *acceptable business casual* for both men and women. Be sure that the descriptions for both genders are balanced.

■ A short list of items that are considered acceptable.

■ A short list of items that are considered unacceptable. Name four or five that are critical for your organization.

■ A short list of the type of accessories that are acceptable, especially shoes and hose.

■ A short list of the type of accessories that are unacceptable.

## B. Defining Specific Policy

Some organizations realize that employees are often confused about what is appropriate and professional business casual clothing. Business casual opens the door to many choices and consequently allows for many mistakes. Therefore, many organizations prefer to define a policy that has more specific guidelines than the ones outlined above to ensure the policy's success and avoid possible mistakes that will affect the company's image. This applies to organizations that tend to be more formal and conservative, such as financial service companies, banks, consulting firms, etc.

If this is the case for your company, in addition to the above considerations for general guidelines, you may want to develop a *draft document* of several pages. Four or five will be sufficient depending on how specific your organization wants to be. To structure this policy you may want to include the following elements:

## 1. Purpose

■ The reasons why your organization is implementing this new way of dressing for work.

■ Considerations about your organization goals and image. If employees have asked for this new way of dress for work, include wording such as *"We've listened to your comments and suggestions…"*

## 2. Timing

■ Days of the week, daily, Fridays, or all-year round, etc.

■ Determine the timing for the policy definition. At the end of this time the people responsible for the project or the task force, if there is one, will produce a document that outlines the company's guidelines for business casual. This document will be polished and presented to the employees according to the guidelines presented in the Information/ Communication step (see page 172).

## 3. Definition

■ Define the guidelines as specifically as possible. Make a list of the guidelines for appearance that the company expects according to the general company's image. Explain the reasons for these guidelines.

■ Include clear and more complete descriptions of what is *appropriate* and what is *not appropriate* for your organization. You may use the guidelines from this book and select the levels that will fit your organization's culture.

■ Explain how the traditional business attire fits into the new casual dress policy and give examples of when it is necessary. If you leave it up to the employees' judgments, it may be misunderstood. Give examples: *"Wearing traditional business attire will be necessary when visiting or meeting with clients, representing the company outside the premises,"* etc.

■ Include a list of items that are *acceptable* for men and a list for women. Include pieces of clothing that you want to see people wearing. A list of 10 to 15 items in each list will be sufficient. Use a format like this:

**Men**

| | |
|---|---|
| Shirts: | Explain sleeve length |
| | • collar or no collar |
| | • type, such as polo, buttoned-down, etc. |
| Jackets: | Blazers, sport coats |
| Sweaters: | Cardigan, turtleneck, etc. |
| Pants: | Include type and fabric such as khaki, twill, cotton, corduroy, denim, etc. |
| Shoes: | Type, sole thickness, heel size (loafers, boots, sneakers, etc.) |
| Socks: | Needed at all times or not |

**Women**

| | |
|---|---|
| Blouses/tops: | Type, sleeve and neck length, tunic tops, polo shirts, etc. |
| Jackets: | Blazers, knit jackets |
| Sweaters: | Type, turtleneck, V-neck, etc. |
| Pants: | Include type and fabric such as: khaki, twill, cotton, stirrup, type of shorts, denim, etc. |
| Shoes: | Type, sole thickness, heel size (loafers, flats) |
| Socks/hose: | Needed at all times or not |

■ Include a list of items that are *unacceptable* for men and a list for women. Include pieces of clothing that you *do not* want to see people wearing. A list of 10 to 15 items in each list will be sufficient. Use a format like this:

**Men**

| | |
|---|---|
| Shirts: | Explain type, sleeves, etc. (T-shirts with messages, sleeveless shirts) |
| Sweaters: | Type (sweatshirts) |
| Pants: | Include type, length, and fabric (shorts, tight pants, leather, denim, corduroy, etc.) |
| Shoes: | Type, sole thickness, heel size (deck shoes, sneakers, hiking boots, cowboy boots, etc.) |
| Socks/hose: | Needed at all times or not |

**Women**

| | |
|---|---|
| Blouses/Tops: | Type, sleeve and neck length, tank tops, bare shoulders, or midriff, etc. |
| Sweaters: | Type (sweatshirts) |
| Pants: | Include type, length, and fabric (type of shorts, tight pants, leather, stretch pants, leggings, denim, corduroy) |
| Shoes: | Type, sole thickness, heel size (deck shoes, sandals, sneakers, boots, open-toe shoes, etc.) |
| Socks/hose: | Needed at all times or not |

## 4. Definite Dos and Don'ts

■ Make a list of Dos and Don'ts including examples. When defining the guidelines, avoid words such as *professional* or *appropriate*. Define each term with examples and characteristics.

■ Be aware that when using the words *appropriate, inappropriate, professional,* and *unprofessional,* some employees may not have a clear idea of what this means in your organization. Therefore include examples.

## C. For All Types of Policies

Present the casual dress as a choice not a mandate or an additional expense. You may want to specify that the organization is not expecting employees to purchase new wardrobes. The Education step is critical because it teaches employees how to achieve a professional casual wardrobe using pieces from their existing business wardrobes and within a budget.

Whether you define general or specific guidelines for your organization policy, it is important to include a section about proper fit, clothing care, and grooming to present a professional image. Include the following general guidelines at the beginning of your document:

   a. Fit/Clothing—pay attention to fit and care of clothing; casual doesn't mean "sloppy."
   b. Criteria—use your daily agenda as your guide for selecting clothing.
   c. Accessories—pay attention to accessories.
   d. Grooming—pay attention to grooming, hair, nails, hygiene, etc.

To facilitate this step, you may want to review other organizations' policies within your industry. Also read the guidelines of each level presented in this book, as well as the results of our survey that summarizes the opinions of top executives on those controversial items. Using magazines and clothing catalogs will help you identify outfits that are appropriate or inappropriate for your organization.

## 2. INFORMATION/COMMUNICATION

Once the policy is defined, it needs to be communicated to the employees. This step is critical since it will determine whether the policy will be presented as a benefit or as another set of rules to follow.

The purpose of this step is to provide information to the entire staff about the new guidelines. Most organizations find that communicating clear guidelines helps to ensure the policy's success.

## Key Elements

### Document
Present the policy as a written memo so that everyone will have a hard copy. This memo needs to state who is endorsing the policy—human resources, the organization president, CEO, etc., depending on your company's structure.

### Language
Write the policy as positive information, using phrasings such as:

*We are pleased to announce our Business Casual Dress Program!*
*You have asked for it, we are giving business casual to you!*

In producing the final document that includes the defined policy, be sure that it is written positively, avoiding authoritative or patronizing language. Otherwise it will defeat the purpose of the policy as a benefit. One of the key reasons for business casual is to improve communication, therefore the presentation of the policy needs to demonstrate the same spirit of open and friendly camaraderie, empowerment, and flow of communication that it is promoting.

Express management's confidence that employees will use good judgment about selecting appropriate casual dress. Invite them to maintain their professional reputation by always dressing in a way that shows respect for themselves, for the organization, and for their clients.

### Questions

Explain the process that employees can follow when they have questions. Should they ask their supervisor? Or HR? Give clear guidelines.

### Methods of Communication

Use all communication channels in your organization, such as staff memos, bulletins, newsletters, voice mail, electronic mail, posters, staff meetings, large presentations, company meetings, etc., or a combination to ensure that everyone gets the message. Incorporate the new policy into existing documents, such as the company employee handbook.

Visual aids are very effective. Place photos or clothing catalog posters with appropriate looks in places where most employees visit, such as copy rooms, cafeteria, lunchroom, etc. Use employees as models for the photos to show the looks that are expected. You may want to include some samples of inappropriate items also. Dos and Don'ts illustrations will be useful. Avoid using employees as models for the Don'ts illustrations. This would not be productive and could embarrass or make people uncomfortable.

Communication by example. Most employees will follow their leaders. Therefore it is critical that managers understand the policy clearly and that they exemplify it, especially in the first stages of the casual dress process.

## 3. EDUCATION

Defining a policy of what is expected is seldom enough to guarantee that all employees will select the right clothing that is both casual and professional. The criteria for selecting the right clothing for the right occasion is a challenge for most employees who are not well versed in this subject.

Providing education and informative sessions to employees about how to implement the new guidelines will facilitate the success of the program and avoid costly and embarrassing mistakes. The Education step includes sessions for employees and special sessions for managers.

The educational sessions for employees will include an explanation and demonstration of the policy and how to implement it into a person's daily life and their wardrobe. It will include what an appropriate business casual look is and what it is not. Seminars, presentations, or personal coaching are critical at this stage. Fashion shows that are educational yet not commercial will be helpful.

Your organization can plan seminars and presentations for employees on the business casual guidelines. Contacting a Professional Image Consultant with experience in Business Casual will make this stage easier and productive. (Contact Business Casual Publications at 703-560-3950 or 914-478-3827 for a list of consultants nearest you.)

A comprehensive session of one to three hours depending on the number of employees and time, may include the objectives and outline described on the following pages.

## Educational Sessions for Employees

### Objectives

The program will be a group presentation that deals with the importance of your personal appearance in business. It will be designed to help participants look competent, credible, and approachable in today's less formal business settings.

It will include your organization's accepted guidelines for an appropriate business casual look. It can be structured for an audience of both men and women, or it can be conducted in separate groups of men and women. This will be a highly visual demonstration that needs to include audience participation, slides, audiovisual materials, and clothing to reinforce the information presented.

### Outline

- The elements of first impressions. Impact of your personal appearance in business.

- Understanding the messages that clothing sends to others: clothing symbols and perceptions.

- Business Casual, the new paradigm. How is it perceived. How it is achieved.

- Understanding the four Cs of business casual: Comfort, Creativity, Communication, Camaraderie.

- The elements of clothing that makes an outfit casual: color, fabric, construction, layers, and accessories.

- One policy does not fit all. The three levels of business casual and their appropriateness: Classic, Smart, and Relaxed.

- When and how to select each business casual level that is accepted in your organization to achieve your business goals.

- Criteria for selecting your clothing, from traditional business to business casual: client contact, meetings, presentations, building rapport, encouraging creativity, etc.

- Using color for your business casual look. The use of color to build credibility and trust.

- Selecting styles, fabrics, prints for your business casual look.

- Selecting the appropriate accessories that say "business" and "casual."

- Building a business casual wardrobe within a budget. Extending your "corporate" wardrobe into your "business casual" wardrobe.

- Guidelines for proper fit and quality construction when selecting standard pieces of clothing.

## Sessions for Managers

Since managers will be viewed as role models, it is critical that they understand and exemplify the casual dress the way the organization wants to see employees mirroring. Therefore you'll want to schedule special educational sessions for managers that may include:

- Answers to all their questions about clarity and appropriateness of the approved casual dress policy.

- How to coach employees who have questions about the policy, and how to give feedback to employees who do not adhere to the policy or are reluctant to apply the accepted guidelines.

- Individual attention to review their personal business casual wardrobe and tips on how to extend their actual wardrobe into their casual wardrobe.

## Working with Clothing Stores—The Pros and Cons

Some organizations contact local clothing stores to do fashion shows for their employees as a way to illustrate the business casual guidelines. This can be a positive resource or can backfire depending on how it is used.

When selecting a store, remember that their goal is to "sell clothing" and they will try to use your invitation for a fashion show as an opportunity to do so. If you are using a store, be sure that they show different price range clothing, otherwise the fashion show may imply that the organization expects employees to purchase new clothing at a certain price range.

Choose a store that will follow your organization's guidelines in selecting the outfits that will be shown in the fashion show. For educational purposes, ask if they will also show garments that are not appropriate for your organization. If so, these items can be shown on hangers not on models.

A key element of a fashion show is to demonstrate how to build a coordinated wardrobe with pieces that are versatile. This teaches participants how they can build their own wardrobe with just a few pieces, using items from their actual business wardrobe.

The other way to use stores is to ask several retailers in your area to provide your organization with discount coupons that you will offer employees as a benefit. This way you are not open to misinterpretation that you expect employees to purchase clothing from a specific store.

The most effective way to use your local stores is to partner them with a Professional Image Consultant who will conduct your educational seminars. The stores will "lend" clothing for demonstration that the image consultant will select and use during the seminars. Having discount coupons at these sessions will be a good addition.

## 4. APPLICATION

Set a reasonable timetable for employees to make the changes necessary to apply the new dress code and appearance guidelines. About four to six months is recommended in order for employees to have time to expand their wardrobes, try the new casual looks, make adjustments, etc.

During this time your organization may want to implement an *Auditing Process* to collect information on the way the policy has been implemented in the different organization areas. It can be done by observing and collecting data on the most common outfits that employees are wearing that are appropriate and by taking notes about those items that are being worn that the company deems unacceptable. This is about *"catching people doing things right"* not a policing activity. The information collected through this step will be valuable for the follow-up step.

## 5. FOLLOW-UP/ENFORCEMENT

After the information, education, and application time, many organizations establish follow-up and enforcement processes as needed. Usually managers will be in charge of this implementation. During this step, managers will provide feedback to employees who need additional guidance.

Generally the employee's immediate supervisor will be the most appropriate person to provide this coaching. If for any reason such as gender, age, race, or other circumstances, this is not the best way to pursue the coaching, the HR department may become a resource. Managers must be careful though that HR doesn't become the *policy police* of people's appearance.

When giving individual feedback to employees, make sure that confusion is the reason the person is not following the guidelines and not other underlying performance issues, such as discontent, frustration in their jobs, or other personal problems.

While providing feedback to an employee, it is important to focus on the outfit and not on the person. You can provide useful feedback and explain the reasons the outfit is not accepted as professional by your organization's standards. Give a *business reason* or possible impact of inappropriate image. Showing visual examples will provide useful ideas to clarify confusion.

The business casual dress guidelines may be revisited annually or twice a year to ensure that employees apply the accepted policy according to the seasons and weather. During the summer months employees may stretch the limits by wearing clothing that is more comfortable and cooler than the guidelines provide. Short skirts, sleeveless tops, no socks, and no hose are common elements to watch for during the warmer months if your organization doesn't allow these items.

HR may develop a set of visual materials with examples of each one of the articles of clothing listed in the policy for acceptable and unacceptable items. These materials can be used by managers to coach employees.

## Summary

As we can see, defining and implementing a casual dress policy is more than writing a memo to the staff. Many organizations complain that their employees took the dress casual policy too far, affecting the company's image and, as a result, they eliminated it completely. Needless to say, those employees now feel that a perk has been taken away, which negatively affects morale.

Most organizations want to ensure that their employees keep the professionalism within the standards of the organization. Following the above steps may take more time and energy, but it will prevent problems and pay dividends.

# Business Casual Guidelines
## Format

Announcement: Use friendly, upbeat language such as: *We are pleased to announce our Business Casual Dress Policy.*

I. **Purpose.** Why you've decided to change/begin/institute a Business Casual Policy.

II. **Timing.** Specify the starting date and, if appropriate, the ending date of the policy. If it will be Monday through Friday, or Monday through Thursday with Friday as "jeans allowed," then detail that here.

III. **Which departments are included.** Explain whether all employees can wear business casual. If not, specify who can and who can't. Can Administrative, Accounting, Customer Service all wear Business Casual? Will the Sales and Marketing Departments only be allowed to wear Business Casual on Fridays or when not seeing clients? Be specific.

IV. **Definition.** Include what is acceptable and unacceptable with examples for each gender. Remember to be consistent with number of examples for each group.

Women—Acceptable Attire        Men—Acceptable Attire
Be specific and include examples  Be specific and include examples

Women—Unacceptable Attire   Men—Unacceptable Attire
Be specific and include examples  Be specific and include examples

V. **Definite Don'ts for Everyone.** Be specific. No sneakers; torn, ripped clothing; T-shirts with inappropriate slogans; no exercise attire.

VI. **Questions.** Let people know who to go to with questions. Will it be their immediate supervisor or someone in human resources?

VII. **Education.** Explain the programs and activities where you will provide information/education on the subject. Give the general schedule. Invite and motivate employees to participate, i.e., schedule seminars on Business Casual presented by Professional Image Consultants who are experts on the subject. Make sessions available to all employees at convenient times to encourage attendance.

VIII. **Follow-Up.** If policy will be evaluated for adjustments, explain the steps that will follow and the timetable.

## Managing the Business Casual Policy Process

**Managers can support policy by:**

- Exemplifying the casual dress policy
- Answering questions from employees about policy
- Coaching employees on interpreting policy
- Enforcing the policy to maintain the firm's high standards

**Coaching/Follow-up/Enforcing Process**

When an employee is not applying the policy appropriately, follow these steps:

1. Identify the Problem—Determine the Issues
   - Outfit that is unacceptable according to the policy: garment type, fabric, accessories, etc.
   - Inappropriate fit
   - Inappropriate grooming
   - Wearing the right clothes for the wrong occasion. Example: wearing business casual (Smart Level) to meet a client for the first time.

2. Meet with Employee
   - Schedule a private meeting with employee when he/she is wearing appropriate attire
   - Explain the reason for meeting
   - Give positive feedback on the outfit worn that day which reflects company policy

3. Ensure Compliance
   - Define the issue and give reasons for inappropriateness
   - Avoid critiquing on personal features or fashion choices
   - Give a business reason behind the policy, if possible

• Review dress policy with employee
• Give suggestions for change: Show examples.

Use expressions such as: "Some of your choices in casual clothing are not in compliance with our business casual policy. For example, the shirt that you wore yesterday without sleeves is considered inappropriate for our organization."

## Feedback: Examples

| Issue | Reason for Unacceptability | Possible Impact on Company's Image |
| --- | --- | --- |
| Collarless shirt | Unacceptable according to our policy | Most organizations in our field require a shirt that has a collar for business casual attire and our company policy requires it also. |
| Sleeveless top | Unacceptable according to our policy | The more skin that is exposed, the less powerful you look. |
| Skirt too short | Unacceptable according to our policy | Unprofessional and distracts from eye contact. |
| Jeans | Unacceptable according to our policy | Outfit too casual for our industry standards. Clients may feel lack of seriousness. |
| Clothes too tight | Inappropriate for organization standards | Not according to our standards. Affects company's image negatively. |
| Clothes in bad condition | Unacceptable according to our policy | Others may interpret unpolished appearance as lack of attention in handling one's job. |

# Bibliography

*Best Impressions in Hospitality*
   Angie Michael
   Impact Publications

*Casual Day Has Gone Too Far*
   Scott Adams
   A Dilbert Book—Andrews and McMeel

*Clothes and the Man*
   Alan Flusser
   Villar Books

*Color with Style*
   Donna Fujii
   Graphic-Sha Publishing Company

*The Complete Guide to Dressing for Workday Casual*
   Dayton's

*Dress Casually for Success for Men*
   Mark Weber and The Van
   Heusen Creative Design Group
   McGraw-Hill

*From Turmoil to Triumph*
   Mitchell Lee Marks, Ph.D.

*Looking Good*
   Nancy Nix-Rice
   Palmer/Pletsch Publications

*Mastering Your Professional Image*
   Diane Parente and Stephanie Peterson
   Parente & Peterson

*The New Professional Image*
   Susan Bixler and Nancy Nix-Rice
   Adams Media Corporation

*The Power of Dress*
   Jacqueline Murray
   A Semiotics Book

*Plus Style*
   Suzan Nanfeldt
   Plume/Penguin

*The Psychology of Fashion*
   Michael R. Solomon
   Lexington Books

*Red Socks Don't Work*
   Ken Karpinski
   Impact Publications

*You Are What You Wear*
   William Thourlby
   Forbes/Wittenburg & Brown

*Work Clothes—Chic Simple Guides*
   Kim Johnson Gross and Jeff Stone
   Alfred A. Knopf, Inc.

## ORDER FORM

## Business Casual Made Easy
### The Complete Guide to Business Casual Dress for Men and Women

- **Fax Orders:** 703-573-8904
- **Telephone Orders only:** 1-800-247-6553
- **Postal Orders:** Business Casual Publications, L.C
  7804 Wincanton Court, Falls Church, VA 22043

Please send me _____ copy(s) of *Business Casual Made Easy,* by Ilene Amiel and Angie Michael, for $14.95 plus $4.00 to cover U.S. shipping and handling. Please add 4.5% sales tax for shipping to Virginia.

**Total Enclosed:** $ _____

Name _____

Company Name _____

Address _____

City _____State _____ Zip_____

Phone _____ Fax _____

**Payment:** ❏ Check   ❏ Visa   ❏ Master Card   ❏ American Express

Card Number: _____   Exp. Date: _____

Signature: _____

**How did you hear about the book?**
❏ Bookstore   ❏ Internet   ❏ Friend/Colleague
❏ Catalog   ❏ Retail Store   ❏ Publication   ❏ Other

For information on Seminars, Presentations, and Teaching Materials contact:
Washington Office: 703-560-3950, New York Office: 914-478-3827
Visit our web site at: www.businesscasualdress.com